Trading Enterprises
in Agriculture

OECD

ORGANISATION FOR ECONOMIC CO-OPERATION AND DEVELOPMENT

ORGANISATION FOR ECONOMIC CO-OPERATION AND DEVELOPMENT

Pursuant to Article 1 of the Convention signed in Paris on 14th December 1960, and which came into force on 30th September 1961, the Organisation for Economic Co-operation and Development (OECD) shall promote policies designed:

- to achieve the highest sustainable economic growth and employment and a rising standard of living in Member countries, while maintaining financial stability, and thus to contribute to the development of the world economy;
- to contribute to sound economic expansion in Member as well as non-member countries in the process of economic development; and
- to contribute to the expansion of world trade on a multilateral, non-discriminatory basis in accordance with international obligations.

The original Member countries of the OECD are Austria, Belgium, Canada, Denmark, France, Germany, Greece, Iceland, Ireland, Italy, Luxembourg, the Netherlands, Norway, Portugal, Spain, Sweden, Switzerland, Turkey, the United Kingdom and the United States. The following countries became Members subsequently through accession at the dates indicated hereafter: Japan (28th April 1964), Finland (28th January 1969), Australia (7th June 1971), New Zealand (29th May 1973), Mexico (18th May 1994), the Czech Republic (21st December 1995), Hungary (7th May 1996), Poland (22nd November 1996), Korea (12th December 1996) and the Slovak Republic (14th December 2000). The Commission of the European Communities takes part in the work of the OECD (Article 13 of the OECD Convention).

Publié en français sous le titre :
LES ENTREPRISES D'ÉTAT DANS LE SECTEUR AGRICOLE

Foreword

This is the final version of a two-part study that was carried out under the Programme of Work for 1999/2000 adopted by the Committee for Agriculture and endorsed by the Trade Committee. Part I proposes a formal framework to analyse the potential impact of state trading enterprises (STEs) on market access and on world export markets. The study highlights some key issues including the heterogeneous nature of state trading enterprises and the imperfectly competitive markets in which many of them operate. These features, combined with the fact that STEs pursue objectives that may be different from private enterprises, suggest that more research is needed to assess actual trade impacts. The authors of Part I are Steve McCorriston, Reader in Agricultural Economics at the University of Exeter in the United Kingdom and Donald McLaren, Associate Professor of Economics at the University of Melbourne in Australia.

Part II of this study describes the activities of state trading enterprises in agriculture in OECD Member countries using a number of criteria pertinent to the issue of potential market or trade distortion. Only objective and factual criteria are retained. A taxonomy or classification is established within each criterion, although an overall taxonomy is not proposed. Mr Oh Kyung-Tae is the principal author of Part II. Statistical assistance was provided by Mr. Stéphane Guillot. Ms Jennifer Fellows also contributed

3

TABLE OF CONTENTS

Box 1. Preamble

Agriculture Ministers adopted a set of shared goals in March 1998, stressing that these goals should be seen as an integrated and complementary whole. Among the shared goals is the further integration of the agro-food sector into the multilateral trading system. In pursuit of that goal, Ministers mandated the OECD to examine ongoing and new agricultural trade and trans-boundary policy issues and their impacts, and to provide analytical support, as appropriate, to the process of agricultural trade liberalisation.

In response, the Committee for Agriculture adopted (and the Trade Committee endorsed) a comprehensive programme of work on agricultural trade policy issues, to be carried out throughout the period 1999-2000 and continuing during the period 2001-2002. The programme of work was carefully designed to incorporate specific agricultural trade policy issues that are of major interest to Member countries of the OECD, but which may also concern non-OECD countries. A wide range of issues arising at the interface of trade and domestic policy is also covered, such as the trade implications of different kinds of agricultural support measures, food safety, food security, rural development and environmental protection policies.

On-going core activities of the Committee for Agriculture such as the annual monitoring of agricultural policies and medium term outlook exercises provide an essential backdrop to the specific trade programme of work, which is being implemented on two broad fronts.

One **major element**, characterised as evaluating and strengthening trade liberalisation, aims to assist policy makers and negotiators as they enter the next round of multilateral trade negotiations on agriculture by:

— assessing in-depth the effects of the URAA on trade, on agricultural policy and on protection levels

— identifying possible impacts on trade and markets of different scenarios for further trade liberalisation

— analysing the effect of trade policy instruments such as export credits or export taxes and restrictions that have not, to date, been disciplined and the trade impacts of food aid and STEs.

The **second major** element of the agricultural trade policy work programme deals with a wide range of issues that arise increasingly at the interface of trade and domestic policy. The following issues will be examined:

— Production and trade impacts of different agricultural policy measures ranging from market price support to different kinds of direct payments and including agri-environmental measures.

(continued)

5

— The concept of multifunctionality and in particular relationships between policies intended to ensure an adequate supply of agriculture's non-food outputs (such as possible contributions to environmental benefits and rural development) and existing or future international commitments with respect to trade.

— Policies that contribute to improving environmental performance in ways that are consistent with agricultural trade liberalisation.

— The implications of trade liberalisation for food security in OECD and selected non-OECD countries.

— Trade aspects of domestic policies in the area of food safety and quality with respect to topical issues such as biotechnology and animal welfare.

— Trade or trans-boundary aspects of competition policy with respect to geographical labels and state trading.

Reflecting the wide range of issues, different methodologies are employed in the implementation of the agricultural trade work programme — analytical, model-based tools are used alongside statistical and descriptive approaches while some issues receive a conceptual treatment. Choice of methodology is determined by data availability and by the nature and complexity of the issues being examined, leading to either quantitative or qualitative results. In a later phase, work will be undertaken to synthesise the main conclusions and policy implications for each of the main elements of the programme.

The present study is a conceptual analysis of state trading in agricultural markets.

PART I

STATE TRADING IN AGRICULTURAL MARKETS
A CONCEPTUAL ANALYSIS[1]

Summary

The new round of WTO negotiations will deal with a number of issues. Some of them, including agriculture, are part of the "built-in" agenda. Among the "new" issues that are likely to be discussed is the status of state trading enterprises, since they are perceived by some to be trade-distorting.

A formal framework is developed to consider concerns relating to the potential impact of state trading enterprises on market access and world export markets. The general conclusion drawn is that more research is needed to adequately assess these impacts, while key issues are the conditions of imperfect competition in which many state trading enterprises operate and their heterogeneous nature.

State trading enterprises have legitimate status within the rules of the GATT/WTO. While they are legally recognised, there are also rules that exist to constrain those of their activities that might, in principle, distort trade, although monitoring difficulties and the unclear definition for state trading enterprises might have an impact on the effectiveness of the rules.

State trading enterprises can play a variety of roles in agricultural markets. There are many different types of state trading enterprises in existence, with different objectives and functions. They exist in developed and developing countries, and can be importers or exporters.

A number of concerns have been expressed over the impact state trading enterprises might have in terms of international trade. Overall, these concerns tend to relate either to the potential state trading enterprises may have to distort trade through anti-competitive effects stemming from the special rights and privileges they are accorded, or to the potential they may have to circumvent Uruguay Round commitments.

A detailed list of these concerns is given in the paper. They can be broken down into issues that are general questions of competitiveness and those that are specific to state trading enterprises. For both groups of issues, some concerns are dealt with in the existing rules, and therefore recourse is available through the Dispute Settlement Mechanism. For those issues not dealt with in the rules, there is a need for empirical research to determine the actual effects of state trading enterprises, rather than their potential ones. The theoretical framework presented in the paper indicates some of the areas needing particular attention due to the variety of outcomes possible. These include the nature of the market, and the nature (particularly the objective function) of the state trading enterprise.

Some proposals have been made in terms of empirically considering the trade effects of state trading enterprises. These include suggestions for the measurement of trade distortion, and proposals for taxonomies ranking state trading enterprises according to their potential impact on trade. However, these proposals run the risk of being overly simplistic and it is difficult to avoid a degree of subjectivity in the criteria chosen.

The benchmark used in any study is of vital importance. In defining such a benchmark, there is a need to separate government policy from the activities of state trading enterprises; to characterise the nature of competition in the markets in which state trading enterprises operate; and to consider the nature of the objectives pursued by state trading enterprises.

The framework developed to consider the case of an importing state trading enterprise generates a number of key points. These include the conclusion that a state trading enterprise cannot distort the domestic market or limit imports in the absence of specific government policy instruments; that the nature of the competition between firms is important; and that a firm's objective function may be as important as its monopoly position or any advantages gained from its position, in terms of determining behaviour.

The framework used to look at exporting state trading enterprises also generated some key points. First, the nature of the objective function is vital in determining the effects of a state trading enterprise in the international market. However, unlike the case for the importer, the exporter can affect the market in the absence of explicit government policies. Secondly, price segmentation between the domestic and world markets is possible. Thirdly, the effects of these two results can be equivalent to those of government policies. Finally, these results change depending on the nature of competitors, as well as the nature of competition in downstream or upstream industries.

The paper concludes with the need for further, empirical research to determine the real effects of state trading enterprises on the world trading system, as opposed to speculation on potential impacts. In particular, two priorities are outlined. The first is the need for more information on the objective functions of state trading enterprises, given their heterogeneous nature. The second is to assess the actual impact of state trading enterprises on domestic and international markets.

Introduction

In the run-up to the forthcoming round of negotiations on trade liberalisation in the World Trade Organisation (WTO), there has been much discussion on the range of topics that are likely to be part of the agenda. While in recent years there has been considerable speculation on the "new" topics that may be covered (e.g. linking trade and competition policy issues, labour standards and so on), much of the agenda will continue with issues already addressed by the Uruguay Round agreement. In this context, part of the "built-in" agenda will deal with agriculture and the fulfilment of obligations undertaken as part of the Uruguay Round Agreement on Agriculture (URAA) specifically relating to market access provisions, export subsidy commitments and disciplines on domestic agricultural support policies (Article 20). However, there are a series of "new" issues that may be specific to the agricultural part of the negotiations. While some of these issues may emerge in due course (for instance, relating to food standards or genetically modified organisms), one "new" issue that has already received attention relates to the existence and activities of state trading enterprises.

State trading enterprises have moved recently from the background to the foreground in agricultural trade discussions between governments. Since the introduction of the Uruguay Round Agreement on Agriculture in 1995, the United States in particular has been anxious to obtain agreement amongst the members of the WTO that the activities of agricultural state trading enterprises be severely curtailed, if not banned altogether. The Agriculture Commissioner of the European Union (EU) has recently come out in support of a review of these activities, being critical of the use of state trading enterprises by Canada and Australia. However, state trading enterprises are legal entities, the activities of which have been defined principally in Article XVII of GATT 1947 and repeated in GATT 1994.[2]

State trading enterprises are perceived by many commentators and governments to distort agricultural markets. Given that state trading enterprises may have been proffered some degree of market power, either in the sale and/or purchase of agricultural products, there is a concern that they have the ability to limit market access to domestic markets or distort competition in export markets. Consequently, even if the liberalisation of agricultural trade could be agreed in the context of the WTO negotiations via the reduction of tariffs, the expansion of tariff-rate quotas and further restrictions on export subsidies, the concern remains that the benefits of such liberalisation may not fully materialise if countries can maintain the role of state trading enterprises. In this context, state trading enterprises are perceived as causing trade distortions equivalent to the effects of more explicit trade policy instruments that are being negotiated in the WTO. Moreover, there is also a concern that certain countries may not have fulfilled their Uruguay Round commitments due to the activities of state trading enterprises that currently dominate their national markets.

Apart from the concerns relating to state trading enterprises among current WTO members, there is also concern about the role of state trading activities among potential members of the WTO. In particular, many potential new members of the WTO had economies previously under the control of central government where state organisations played a dominant role. In this regard, concern has been expressed about the potential membership of countries previously constituting the former Soviet Union and China, among others. Although many, if not most, of these countries have initiated a programme of privatisation, in many countries seeking accession to the WTO, state trading enterprises may still play a prominent role. Moreover, several of these countries are significant exporters and importers of agricultural products from world markets and there is an expectation that the role of state trading enterprises may be an important issue in the accession negotiations of several of these countries.

Given the perception that state trading enterprises are likely to be harmful to international trade and that, if they are allowed to persist, the potential gains from trade reform may be more limited than they otherwise would be, proposals have already emerged on how to deal with the state trading issue in the forthcoming WTO negotiations. These range from calculating the tariff-equivalent effect of state trading enterprises in importing countries and, with respect to exporting countries, the export subsidy equivalence of their impact on world export markets. An alternative proposal relates to 'ranking' state trading enterprises according to their likely harmful effect on export markets and access to domestic markets. The principle of these options has some merit, although care should be taken in their implementation to avoid some potential deficiencies. These include the danger of oversimplification of the issue of state trading, and in particular a lack of attention to the market environment in which many state trading enterprises operate, and the variety of objectives they may pursue. For a full analysis of the issue of state trading enterprises the focus must go beyond the monopoly or monopsony status associated with them. That said, taxonomies can offer a clear and systematic framework for the empirical information needed for further analysis of the potential trade effects of state trading enterprises. As well, organising the information about state trading enterprises in some way allows for comparisons to be made between them, although a degree of caution is required when doing this. The inventory and taxonomy prepared by the OECD Secretariat (Part II) shows the usefulness, at least initially, of this approach when managing and comparing the large number of factors associated with state trading enterprises.

The purpose of this report is to contribute to the state trading debate by considering in a formal yet transparent framework the issues that arise with respect to the potential impact of state trading activities on market access and world export markets. In general, research — both theoretical and empirical — on state trading enterprises is remarkably thin and the overall conclusion of this report is that more research is required if the state trading issue is to be appropriately addressed in the context of the WTO negotiations. Particular emphasis is given to the choice of the appropriate benchmark for gauging the impact of state trading enterprises. Much of the current debate assumes that agricultural markets are perfectly competitive and that state trading enterprises alone serve to distort this picture. However, there is considerable evidence from the academic literature that agricultural markets may be more appropriately characterised as being imperfectly competitive. If correct, this raises the question regarding the likely impact of a state trading enterprise if it competes with a limited number of private traders. Moreover, state trading enterprises are heterogeneous in nature and follow a variety of objectives. As will be shown, the nature of these objectives can be an important concern if the impact of state trading activity is to be fully addressed.

This study first describes the status of state trading enterprises in the WTO, the range of activities they carry out and their incidence. The kinds of concerns that have been raised about possible competition or trade distortions are then outlined, both with respect to state trading enterprises in general and those engaged in agriculture in particular. Different possibilities for analysing the activities of STEs are then explored. The analytical framework proposed is then elaborated for importing and exporting STEs. The study ends with an assessment of the different concerns that have been raised concerning STEs and with some suggestions for further research in this area.

The status of state trading enterprises in the WTO

The issue of state trading has long been recognised in the GATT framework and the WTO has endorsed state trading enterprises as legitimate partners in trade. However, while state trading enterprises are legitimate participants in trade, the original 1947 agreement attempted to regulate their behaviour in accordance with general GATT rules. It was understood from the inception of the GATT (1947) that state trading enterprises had the potential to distort trade unless they were also bound by rules imposed by certain of the Articles. In general, the Articles of the GATT are premised on the existence of market economies in which firms make decisions based upon economic principles and not upon government instruction (Davey, 1998). Specifically, Article XVII addressed the state trading issue whereby state trading enterprises (i) were subject to the GATT principle of non-discrimination and most-favoured nation treatment (Article I), and (ii) should act on the basis of "commercial considerations" (Interpretative Note to Article XVII). Further, Article II:4 states that, in the case of state trading enterprises in importing countries, they should not maintain mark-ups higher than the tariff levels bound in GATT.

Restrictions on the behaviour of state trading enterprises are not limited to Articles I, II and XVII. State trading enterprises are also mentioned in Article III (National Treatment on Internal Taxation and Regulation), Ad Article XI (General Elimination of Quantitative Restrictions), Ad Article XII (Restrictions to Safeguard the Balance of Payments), Article XIII (Non-discriminatory Administration of Quantitative Restrictions), Article XIV (Exceptions to the Rule of Non-discrimination), Article XVI (Subsidies) and Article XVIII (Governmental Assistance to Economic Development), in terms of import or export restrictions made effective through state trading operations. Therefore, the activities of state trading enterprises which have the potential to distort international trade are very obviously constrained, at least in principle and in practice by the extent that monitoring is possible, by many of the Articles of the GATT.

One of the main problems with the GATT Articles attempting to control the behaviour of state trading enterprises is that they did not fully clarify what was meant by a "state trading enterprise". Early GATT rules referred to state enterprises that had been granted "formally, or in effect, exclusive or special privileges" but also made reference to "any enterprise under the jurisdiction of a contracting party". However, following the Uruguay Round Agreement in 1994, Article XVII was maintained but an attempt was made to define precisely what was meant by a "state trading enterprise". The *Understanding on the Interpretation of Article XVII of the General Agreement on Tariffs and Trade 1994* defines a state trading enterprise as:

"Governmental and non-governmental enterprises, including marketing boards, which have been granted exclusive or special rights or privileges, including statutory or constitutional powers, in the exercise of which they influence through their purchases or sales the level or direction of imports or exports." (WTO 1995a, p. 25)

As well as outlining some general rules regarding the activities of state trading enterprises as they affect trade, there was an attempt to enhance transparency regarding the incidence and activities of state traders through a notification procedure. This was a self-reporting exercise whereby GATT signatories had to provide information (due every three years) on state trading enterprises under their jurisdiction. To aid the process, each member had to respond to a questionnaire, developed originally in 1960, which requested information regarding: (i) the enumeration of state trading enterprises and the products covered, (ii) the reasons for introducing and maintaining state trading enterprises, (iii) the functions of the enterprise, (iv) provide some statistical information, and (v) if relevant, explain why no foreign trade had taken place.

Despite the best of intentions, this self-reporting procedure has not been noted for its success. First of all, the response rate has been generally poor. Ingco and Ng (1998) report that, between 1980 and 1994, only 45 countries submitted notifications with only three countries providing notifications for every notification period. Following the 1990 and 1993 requests for notification, a total of only 18 countries had responded and only five countries had responded to both requests for information. Of these 18 countries, three reported no state trading enterprises in existence. Even then, the reporting procedure was disappointing as, in several cases, the information provided by the respondents was not specific enough to fully ascertain the importance of state trading enterprises. For example, with respect to product coverage, this was not detailed for each specific state trading enterprise. Further, the questions were only selectively answered and the responses were frequently incomplete. However, perhaps the most significant problem with the 1960 questionnaire that contributed to the lack of success of this self-reporting mechanism was that there was clearly some confusion as to what constituted a state trading enterprise and what was meant by "exclusive rights and privileges".

As discussed above, following the completion of the Uruguay Round in 1994, there was an attempt to provide greater clarity as to what constituted a state trading enterprise. Furthermore, a WTO working party on state trading was established, one of the tasks of which was to review the adequacy of the 1960 questionnaire. On the basis of the subsequent review, the questionnaire was revised in April 1998. Whilst in principal the new questionnaire is similar to its 1960 precursor, including the principle of self-reporting, the revised version provides more detailed instructions on the information to be provided. In order to ensure that the operation of state trading enterprises are as transparent as possible, in the *Understanding on the Interpretation of Article XVII of the General Agreement on Tariffs and Trade 1994*, members agreed (paragraph 2) that they would notify the Council for Trade in Goods of their state trading enterprises using a questionnaire (most recently revised in April 1998) and that these would be monitored by the Working Party on state trading enterprises. Such notification is to cover all state trading enterprises whether or not imports or exports actually occurred during the reporting period. Moreover, all members of the WTO are obliged to respond whether or not use is made of state trading enterprises.

The information to be reported via the questionnaire includes a description of the products covered by the country's state trading enterprises, the reason for the existence of the state trading enterprise, the legal basis for granting the exclusive right or privilege, a description of the functioning of the state trading enterprise, and statistical information on imports, exports and domestic production. The notification is to be made annually and on a three-year cycle (WTO document series G/STR/N/--). In the first year, the notification is to be comprehensive; in the next two years, updated information has to be provided indicating any changes. For countries that do not use state trading enterprises, these steps in reporting have still to be followed. The annual notifications are made available to all members for scrutiny and questions may be asked by members of each other and answers provided. Written questions and answers are all in the public domain (WTO document series G/STR/Q1/--). In addition, if a member believes that a notification is incomplete or wrong, then a counter-notification may be made. In general, the notification procedure has been partially improved with WTO members now taking the self-reporting mechanism more seriously. The number of respondents has increased and the quality of the responses has also improved. Of the 134 current members of the WTO, 76 countries have responded to the questionnaire as of August 1999. Of these 76 countries, 33 report no state trading enterprises in existence with 43 reporting the existence of one or more state trading enterprises. All 29 OECD Members responded to the questionnaire, with 14 reporting the existence of at least one state trading enterprise. A more complete description of these notifications can be found in Part II.

That said, however, some problems appear to remain with the notification procedure. In particular, there are still a large number of countries (58) that have yet to respond to the questionnaire, and some confusion still exists regarding the interpretation of what constitutes a state trading enterprise. For example, Ackerman and Dixit (1997) note that some countries reported the absence of any state trading enterprise despite the fact that they were known to exist. To some degree, there may still be confusion as to what constitutes "exclusive and special privileges" particularly when the state trading enterprise may compete with private sector enterprises. The extent of non-notification and the varied interpretation as to what is meant by "exclusive and special privileges" would suggest that further clarification as to what is defined as a "state trading enterprise" may be warranted.

The role of state trading enterprises in agricultural markets

State trading in agriculture covers both developed and developing countries and importing and exporting countries. The types of state trading enterprise vary across countries and the WTO has classified them into seven groups of which only five are relevant to agricultural products (WTO 1995*b*, pp. 3-14). *Statutory marketing boards* are the most common type and are important for grains (mainly wheat) and dairy products. Their principal activities appear to be domestic price stabilisation and regulation, income support for producers and the control of trade. *Export marketing boards* tend to be more independent of government than statutory marketing boards and are often assumed to pursue profit-maximising strategies in international markets. *Regulatory marketing boards* tend not to trade directly but they influence trade through setting prices or quantities of traded goods. *Canalising agencies* are found in developing countries. Their aims are to achieve economies of scale (bulk discounts on imports and higher prices for exports) in trading operations through restricting imports and/or exports through specific channels. *Foreign trade enterprises/organisations* are a feature of non-market economies and, as such, are much less important now than previously. They hold monopoly rights on international trade transactions. Part II further describes the classification system used by the WTO, along with some other possible categorisations for the different state trading enterprises.

On the basis of the notifications to the Council for Trade in Goods, the objectives of state trading enterprises appear to include:

- income support for domestic producers;

- price stabilisation;

- expansion of domestic output;

- continuity of domestic food supply;

- increase in government revenue;

- control of foreign trade operations, achieving economies of scale and scope, and improving the terms of trade;

- protection of public health;

- management of domestic resources; and

- fulfilment of international commitments on quantity and/or price (WTO 1995*b*, page 3).

In some instances, state trading enterprises have recently become more commercially orientated and to this list of objectives could be added that of maximising returns to producers through achieving economies of scale in marketing.

In order to achieve these objectives, state trading enterprises carry out a number of functions that vary from country to country and from one state trading enterprise to another. These include:

- importing and exporting;

- issuing permits for importation or exportation;

- enforcing the statutory requirements of an agricultural marketing scheme and/or stabilisation arrangement;

- authorising and/or management of domestic production;

- authorising and/or managing the processing of domestic production;

- determining the purchase price of domestic production and/or sales price of domestic production;

- handling domestic distribution of domestic production and/or imports;

- effecting purchases and sales of domestic production based upon pre-determined floor and ceiling prices;

- issuing credit guarantees for producers and/or processors;

- engaging in exporting activities and supporting activities (e.g. storage, shipping, processing, packing and insurance);

- exercising quality control functions for exports;

- engaging in marketing and promotional activities for exports and/or domestic consumption;

- maintaining emergency stocks of certain strategic and/or agricultural goods;

- negotiating and/or administering long-term bilateral contracts for exports and/or imports; and

- undertaking activities necessary to fulfil contractual obligations entered into by government (WTO 1995b, pp. 21-22).

The incidence of state trading enterprises

Despite the recognition in principle about the existence and activities of state trading enterprises in the WTO framework, there is only limited information on the incidence of state trading enterprises in the world economy. A relatively recent UNCTAD report (UNCTAD, 1990) reported the existence of 546 state trading enterprises across 90 developing countries. Although not specifically related to trade, but indicative of the importance of the state in economic activity, the World Bank reports that the state sector accounts for around 13% of GDP across a wide range of developing economies. Schmitz (1996) argues that this figure is higher if one focuses on manufacturing GDP noting that most state intervention in developing countries occurs in this sector. Although privatisation has spread among developing countries, the impression remains that state trading enterprises are likely to be prevalent among developing countries. State trading also exists among developed countries. Although their role in the manufacturing sector is relatively limited, state trading is common in the services sector (e.g. telecommunications) and, in particular, agriculture. For example, McCalla and Schmitz (1982) note that, in the world grains market, in the late 1970s in around 90% of transactions at least one party was characterised as a state trading enterprise.

State trading in agriculture covers both developed and developing countries and importing and exporting countries. With the exception of the European Union (which has not notified the commodity management committees as a "state trading enterprise"), all of the main exporters and importers of agricultural goods use state trading enterprises to manage their agricultural trade. Most notable state trading countries on the export side include the United States (which has notified the Commodity Credit Corporation as a state trading entity), Canada (the Canadian Wheat Board), Australia (the Australian Wheat Board and the Queensland Sugar Corporation among others), and New Zealand (the New Zealand Dairy Board among others). On the import side again most of the major importers of agricultural commodities (excluding the European Union) have notified the WTO that they use state trading enterprises. Included on this list are: the United States (the Commodity Credit Corporation), Japan (the Japanese Food Agency), Indonesia (Badan Urusan Logistick or BULOG) and South Korea (the Ministry of Agriculture and Forestry and the Livestock Products Marketing Organisation among others). Many of these state trading enterprises are responsible for the importation of more than one commodity. For example, South Korea lists eight state trading enterprises responsible for around 18 commodities.

While state trading enterprises are prevalent in the agricultural sector among current WTO members, a further concern with state trading enterprises relates to their role among non-WTO countries. This is a WTO issue insofar as many of these countries are due to seek WTO membership. Many formerly centrally-planned economies of Eastern Europe are known to have a high presence of state trading enterprises. Notable in this regard is the Russian Federation and the Ukraine which are both potentially significant players in world agricultural markets and where national and regional governments control domestic procurement and, to varying degrees, export and import transactions. However, the country that causes most concern for WTO members is China where state trading plays a dominant role over a wide-range of agricultural exports and imports. The China National Cereals, Oil and Foodstuffs Import and Export Corporation (COFCO) is responsible for the import and export of a wide range of Chinese agricultural imports and exports. Further, given China's growing importance on world agricultural markets, COFCO can have a potentially significant impact on world markets.

The concern with state trading enterprises

General

It is clear from the above discussion of GATT rules that state trading enterprises are seen as legitimate partners in trade while Article XVII attempts to influence their behaviour. However, what particular concerns may arise with respect to state trading activities? Consider more closely the WTO definition of "state trading enterprises" reported above. There are two key points to note. First, it is not ownership *per se* that matters but the extent to which any organisation has been bestowed "exclusive or special rights" by the government. Second, it is the nature of these exclusive rights and how the exercise of those exclusive rights impact on trade which is the central concern of the state trading issue.

In this regard, there are six potentially anti-competitive effects that may arise from the exercise of such exclusive rights: (i) that, as a consequence, the exclusive rights create a dominant position that may inhibit market access for foreign competitors; (ii) in addition to the monopoly power, exclusive rights may create monopsony power; (iii) that state trading enterprises can more easily discriminate among trading partners with respect to prices and quality standards; (iv) that, insofar as the exclusive rights create enterprises with "single desk status", i.e. enterprises with responsibility for domestic and export sales, state trading enterprises may be able to cross-subsidise sales in export markets; (v) due to ties with governments, there may be hidden subsidies or other advantages that would not be available to private firms; and (vi) state trading enterprises may not be concerned with bankruptcy which may give them an advantage over private companies. This list of potential concerns is general and not specific to agriculture. Nevertheless, there is a range of potential issues arising with respect to state trading activities in agricultural markets more directly. These are highlighted below.

State trading issues with respect to agricultural trade

The main argument put forward by those who wish to ban agricultural state trading enterprises is that they are "unfair traders" which distort international trade in agricultural products, particularly in cereals and dairy products, and that that they have the potential to circumvent the provisions of the URAA. This potential arises with respect to Tariff-Rate Quotas (TRQs) (paragraph 5, Annex 3 in *Modalities for the Establishment of Specific Binding Commitments under the Reform Programme*) and export subsidies (Articles 9 and 10 of the URAA). Several authors, e.g. Ackerman (1997 and 1998), Dixit and Josling (1997) and Ingco and Ng (1998), list ways in which state trading enterprises have the potential to circumvent or to corrupt the operation of TRQs and also to subsidise exports at levels which are in breach of the constraints imposed by the Agreement. This is an empirical issue but, to date, there is a noted absence of even anecdotal evidence let alone precise and documented information. In a domestic setting, agricultural state trading enterprises are not usually subject to nations' competition policies and, hence, they are legitimate (anti-competitive) entities within national boundaries.

There are two separate issues to investigate with respect to the legality of the activities of state trading enterprises. First, it needs to be established whether in practice agricultural state trading enterprises violate the Articles of GATT, principally Article XVII. If they do so in specific circumstances, then the Dispute Settlement procedures are potentially available to members to halt the violation. If state trading enterprises do not violate the relevant GATT Articles, then the only grounds for protest are their actual, rather than their potential, evasion of the rules specified in the URAA. Second, in the latter case, and applying the concept of the "targeting rule" from the theory of international trade policy, the remedy lies in removing the distortion at source rather than indirectly, i.e. removing the TRQs as an instrument of market opening and banning export subsidies for agricultural products, rather than banning state trading enterprises which have a legal status within the WTO. As we discuss below, separating trade distortions due to government policies as distinct from those due to the activities of state trading enterprises should be a key factor in dealing with the state trading issue.

Several commentators have linked the state trading issue with the obligations by member countries to fulfil the URAA commitments on reducing levels of support in the agricultural sector (for example, Ingco and Ng, 1998) and market access. It will be recalled that the outcome of the URAA was to convert all non-tariff barriers into tariff equivalents (which would be bound) and to promote market access via tariff-rate quotas in order to guarantee a (rising) level of market access into importing countries. The suspicion against countries with state trading enterprises is that the institutional arrangements can somehow allow them to circumvent their Uruguay Round commitments, particularly with regard to market access. It is necessary, however, to be specific about the issues in this case. Consider, first of all, that the URAA introduced greater transparency into the levels of agricultural support among WTO members. Non-tariff barriers have been converted to tariff equivalents and the resulting tariffs bound. Note also that there is increasing transparency arising from WTO members' notifications of state enterprises in that, as discussed above, importing countries have to record the mark-up of domestic prices over import prices for products covered by the state trading enterprise. Thus, at least in principle, it is relatively straightforward to compare whether the level of the mark-up exceeds the bound tariff rate. If state trading enterprises are therefore a problem, it relates to their ability to circumvent this two-stranded reporting procedure. For example, this would require them to reduce the mark-up that they report to the WTO under the notification process while still limiting the degree of market access to their markets. It should, nevertheless, be borne in mind that a large number of countries have yet to respond to the WTO questionnaire.

A second suspicion associated with state trading enterprises relates to the management of TRQs This mechanism is an attempt to ensure a certain level of market access to importing country markets. In many countries, this is done by some sort of licensing scheme. However, in some countries, the tariff-rate quota is managed by a state trading enterprise, i.e. state trading enterprises do not have direct responsibility for imports but rather issue licences to private traders. Indeed, some countries (e.g. the Philippines) have established state trading enterprises with the sole purpose of managing the import arrangements agreed through the Uruguay Round. The suspicion arises that the rate of quota utilisation (or fill rates) will be influenced by the existence of state trading enterprises and hence market access will be limited and the Uruguay Round commitments will not be fulfilled.

However, whether the rate of quota utilisation will be less with a state trading enterprise compared to an alternative licensing scheme is debatable since alternative import licensing arrangements do not guarantee a higher rate of quota fill. For example, import licences can be auctioned or allocated to importing or exporting firms by given criteria (e.g. first-come, first served or by historical status as importer and so on, and allocated by broad commodity group or be product specific and country specific) with the extent of competition in the licence market determining the rate of quota fill. There is no *a priori* reason why the institutional arrangements are more important than the allocative mechanism or that state trading enterprises should, on their own, result in a lower rate of quota utilisation. The WTO has identified ten methods of allocation of tariff-rate quotas, each of which has generated different fill rates. These ranged in 1995 from 32% for auctioning of the right to import to 82% for allocation based on historical shares (ABARE 1999, Table 6a). The average fill rate for state trading enterprises was 80% in 1995 and 82% in 1996. The experience thus far with the 36 countries and 1 370 tariff-rate quotas is that, on average, the quotas are not being filled. These figures are confirmed by a report on market access prepared by the OECD. However, as the quota fill by state trading enterprises is among the highest of any method used, the reason behind low fill rates most likely lies elsewhere.

A third concern relates to whether countries with state trading enterprises offer higher rates of protection compared with non-state trading countries. The (albeit limited) empirical evidence, however, shows that there is no reason to suspect that state trading countries have higher levels of protection than those characterised by private traders. Using data for 23 wheat importing countries for the period 1980-1994, Young and Abbott (1998) found no conclusive evidence that state trading importing countries were associated with relatively higher levels of protection. While the average effective tariff was higher over state trading importers (largely due to presence of Iran, Japan and Brazil in the sample), this was not significantly different from the average level of protection in importing countries where the private sector is involved in importing wheat. As Abbott and Young suggest, what is more relevant to the analysis of protection in the agricultural sector is to identify what the government policy is and not what the institutional arrangements are *per se*. This applies equally to the link between state trading and Uruguay Round commitments.

Anti-competitive behaviour by state trading enterprises

Many of the concerns about state trading enterprises are associated with the way in which they may affect competition on world markets. These concerns are generally voiced in relation to the specific case of single buyers or sellers. In the case of state trading importers, the issue is clear-cut. If the state trading enterprise controls domestic procurement and sales and determines the level of imports, then this is a market access issue for exporting countries. It is more elusive to identify the (anti)-competitive effects related to the activities of state trading exporters. While the Uruguay Round commitments also pertain to the use of export subsidies, in many cases, state trading exporters do not explicitly subsidise their exports to world markets. The concern in this case, therefore, must be that the 'commercial' behaviour of the state trading enterprise and/or the nature of its ties with the government can influence its performance in world export markets at the expense of non-state trading exporters. In other words, aspects of this behaviour, e.g. cross-subsidisation across countries, commodities or across time periods, have effects that are *equivalent* to export subsidies (or, in some cases, export taxes).

In order to offer a concrete illustration of the complicated nature of the issues of state trading enterprises in general, and exporting state trading enterprises in particular, Table I.1 summarises some features of the state trading activities of the Canadian Wheat Board and the Australian Wheat Board which can (it is hypothesised) influence their behaviour on the world wheat market. There are several potential issues that arise from the above characterisation. First, both wheat boards control both exports and account for a high proportion of domestic procurement of domestic wheat production and hence in effect for (most of) domestic sales (they have "single-desk" status). They therefore have the potential to price discriminate (or cross-subsidise sales) between domestic and foreign markets (although it should be noted that price discrimination by state trading enterprises is legitimate under GATT Article XVII, being a normal commercial activity).[3] The potential for and gains from price discrimination will depend on the effectiveness of market segmentation and the nature of market access in importing countries. For example, the use of tariffs or tariff-rate quotas or other barriers to trade will be a factor in determining market access and hence the gains from price discrimination in foreign markets. In addition, the openness of the exporting country's market to imports will determine domestic prices and how they differ from export prices. For example, under the North American Free Trade Arrangement (NAFTA), imports from the United States and Mexico can enter Canada duty-free and hence may have an impact on the degree to which countries can benefit from price discrimination. In the Australian case, segmentation and the opportunities to price discriminate are more complete because imports of wheat are banned by quarantine regulations. Related to the price discrimination, is the practice of price pooling. In broad terms, price pooling involves paying producers an average price from sales in all markets. However, the practice of price pooling may be more subtle. Specifically, in the case of the Canadian Wheat Board, producers receive an initial payment that is equivalent to 70-80% of final price. Additional payments are made to producers at a later date when the total supply of the commodity has been marketed. However, the initial pool payments are guaranteed by the Canadian government such that, if the pooled price is below the initial price paid to producers, it will underwrite the Wheat Board's losses. Clearly, as the United States has again argued, this may give an advantage to Canadian exporters that would not be available if the exports were undertaken by the private sector. However, government guarantees in Canada have been rarely utilised. Note, in addition, that since 1989 the Australian government has not underwritten the guaranteed minimum producer price. However, until June 1999, it continued to underwrite the losses of its Wheat Board, and producers were levied and the accumulated monies placed in the Wheat Industry Fund which the AWB could use to underwrite its commercial activities. Moreover, given that the Canadian government may under-write the activities of the Canadian Wheat Board, loans to it are perceived as lower risk and are hence less costly. Finally, note that neither country uses export subsidies as policy instruments. However, the criticism of these state trading exporters appears to be that there are hidden benefits owing to their ties with the central government and/or its single-desk status whereby they can account for both most of domestic and all of foreign sales, and can have an effect equivalent to the use of explicit export subsidies.

Table I.1. Characteristics of the Canadian and Australian Wheat Boards

Characteristic	Canadian Wheat Board	Australian Wheat Board
Control of Exports	100%	100%
Export Share of Production	68%	72 %
Domestic Procurement	100%	86% (but no exclusive authority)
Policy Instruments		
Export Subsidies	None	None
Domestic Supply Control	Delivery Contracts	None
Domestic Pricing	Price Pooling	Price Pooling
Government Guarantees	Available	Previously available, now reformed

N.B. The information relates to wheat only. In both cases, the boards are responsible for a wider range of commodities. For example, the CWB has an export monopoly on barley and the AWB is permitted to trade in other grains.
Source: Ackerman (1997) with adaptation. The figures in the table are sourced from WTO notifications, 1995-97.

Proposed options for analysing state trading issues

Measuring the trade-distorting impact of state trading enterprises

As discussed above, the concern with state trading enterprises is that they may distort international markets, both in terms of market access to import markets and anti-competitive practices on export markets, even if the state trading enterprise in question does not explicitly use an identifiable trade policy instrument. As a consequence, there have been suggestions that the trade-distorting effect could be measured with a view to highlighting and subsequently reducing the impact of state trading enterprises' impact on agricultural markets. The general presumption behind this idea is that the impact of state trading activities is indeed measurable, an idea that has had a long history (Lloyd, 1982). For example, in the case of a state trading enterprise in an importing country, the idea would be to measure the tariff-equivalent of the mark-up due to the restricted market access allowed to foreign suppliers. With knowledge (or appropriate assumptions) concerning the import demand schedule and the export supply schedule (which would be perfectly elastic in the small-country, perfectly competitive case), a tariff equivalent measure of the state trading activity could, in principle, be derived. Similarly, with appropriate knowledge or assumptions relating to the world market, the export subsidy or export tax equivalent impact could be derived.

Recent papers which have discussed this approach in the context of the current debate on state trading activities in agricultural markets include Ingco and Ng (1998) and Dixit and Josling (1997). Both of these papers present a simplified framework that is intended to capture the characteristics of state trading enterprises in importing and exporting markets and which attempt to allow for market power exerted by the state trading enterprise. We discuss issues relating to the appropriate framework for analysing state trading activities below. Suffice to note at present that Dixit and Josling foresee the principal barrier to this option being the empirical information necessary to calculate these trade instrument equivalent measures.

Ranking state trading enterprises

This proposal is similar in intent to the tariff and export subsidy equivalent approach without the measurement. In other words, the attempt here is to *qualitatively rather than quantitatively* rank the likely "most distorting" state trading enterprises from the "least distorting" ones according to some objective criteria. In doing so, this would create an inventory of state trading enterprises according to their trade-distorting effect. This has been the approach suggested by Dixit and Josling (1997) where they attempt to rank state trading enterprises by type with "Type 1" being "least trade distorting" to "Type 4" being the "most trade-distorting". The presumption is that state trading activities across countries are highly variable and that the WTO negotiations should focus on those state trading enterprises that cause most harm. Dixit and Josling outline a range of criteria for undertaking this ranking including: trade balance, "market control" (i.e. whether the state trading enterprise is involved in domestic procurement and/or domestic sales), the "policy regime", product range covered by the state trading enterprise and its ownership and management structure. Using these criteria, Dixit and Josling place the Canadian Wheat Board and Indonesia's BULOG in the "Type 4" box or "most trade-distorting" category.

One obvious criticism of this approach relates to the objectivity of the criteria used to rank state trading enterprises by their trade distorting impact. For example, Veeman et al. (1999) use alternative criteria based broadly on how "contestable" a particular market is likely to be. Specifically, the criteria for ranking the trade distorting impact of state trading enterprises are given as the extent of competition that state trading enterprises face from private traders in export markets, the existence of single-desk status (i.e. the level of competition on the domestic market from private traders), the share of the state trading enterprise in export markets (or, alternatively, import markets) and, in the case of an exporting country with a state trading enterprise, the openness of export country's market to imports. By this range of criteria, Veeman *et al.* place the Canadian Wheat Board in the "least-trade distorting" category (i.e. their "green" box) with the state trading enterprises in Japan and Korea being placed in their "red" box. The observation to be made here is that in the quest to rank state trading enterprises by their likely impact on agricultural markets, the selection criteria may be subject to criticism and open to dispute in the absence of any consensus on determining objective criteria. In particular, the debate on state trading has not considered the appropriate "benchmark" against which to gauge the impact of state traders. As the discussion below shows, dealing with the state trading problem is not just a question of data but a lack of economic research (both theoretical and empirical) in defining more accurately the environment in which state trading activities operate.[4]

There are several considerations which generally have been lacking from the recent literature on state trading enterprises and the attempts to deal with their impact on world agricultural markets. Specifically, these include: (i) the need to separate central government's determination of agricultural policy (regarding, for example, the level and forms of price support and trade policy instruments) from the activities of state trading enterprises; (ii) characterising the nature of competition in the markets in which state trading enterprises operate; and (iii) the nature of the objectives pursued by the state trading enterprises. We address these issues in turn.

A casual observer to the current debate on state trading enterprises in agricultural markets may be led to believe that the distortions in many countries are due solely to the nature of state trading. While it may be the case that state trading has a trade-distorting impact, it is nevertheless important to separate what the state trading enterprise does from general government policy towards the agricultural sector. In a large number, if not most, cases, the trade distorting impact originates from the levels of domestic prices and the choice of policy instruments that are set by the government, not the state trading enterprise *per se*. For example, in the case of Japan it is the central government, not the Japanese Food Agency, that sets internal prices and determines quota levels. The state trading enterprise is therefore only the instrument of government policy for administering imports and not necessarily the main cause of the world market distortions. Similarly, in the case of COFCO in China with which some concern has been expressed, it is the Chinese central government that determines the country's import requirements, not the state trading agency. As Young and Abbott (1998) concluded from their study in comparing the levels of protection between state and non-state trading countries, identifying the impact of state trading enterprises on world markets may be less important than determining the impact of the central government's (or state governments') agricultural policies. It is clearly important to distinguish between the two.[5]

A second issue relates to the nature of the competitive environment in which state trading enterprises operate. Much of the recent debate implicitly assumes that the only distortion to competition in agricultural markets arises from the existence and practices of state trading enterprises. Moreover, in the review of the options currently proposed to deal with the state trading issue, the economic models used explicitly assume that market power is solely in the hands of the state trading enterprise and that it competes in a competitive environment. However, there is considerable evidence to suggest that this is not the case although it should be acknowledged that much of this evidence arises from studies of the world wheat market. The first study of note was by McCalla (1966) who suggested that the world wheat market should be characterised as a duopoly (between the United States and Canada). Subsequent studies by, among others, Alouze, Sturgess and Watson (1978), Karp and McCalla (1983), Kolstad and Burris (1986), Love and Murningtyas (1992), and Abbott and Kallio (1996), contribute to the overall impression that characterising world agricultural markets as perfectly competitive may be misleading. There is also evidence from studies by Pick and Park (1991) and Pick and Carter (1994) that there exists "pricing-to-market" with respect to specific destinations for U.S. wheat exports. This finding is not consistent with perfect competition. A further piece of evidence that again is not consistent with perfect competition are the activities of importing state trading enterprises which may try to minimise their exposure to import volume risk and price risk by adopting a portfolio approach to importing with respect to alternative import sources [for example, Alston *et al.* (1990) and Carter (1992)]. Moreover, even casual observation would at least question the perfectly competitive assumption; most trade in cereals is accounted for by five American multinational firms (including Cargill, Louis Dreyfus and Continental). Veeman *et al.* (*op cit.*) make much of this observation in exploring the potential impact of the Canadian Wheat Board on world markets. The central point is that in identifying the anti-competitive impact of state trading enterprises it is necessary to identify who its major competitors are.

A third consideration in defining the benchmark against which to identify the impact of state trading relates to the nature of the state trading enterprises' objective function. In almost all of the discussion to date, the anti-competitive impact of state trading enterprises has focused on their monopoly status. At one level this focus is correct: by definition, the exclusive rights and privileges conferred on state trading enterprises ensures that there is only one organisation that operates in the domestic market. It appears that much of the concern with state trading enterprises arises from this monopoly status. However, in moving from observation to analysis, the presumption made is that the state trading enterprise behaves like a private monopolist. In other words, it is assumed, at least implicitly, that the state trading enterprise is solely concerned with maximising its economic rent. However, this confuses form (i.e. monopoly) with behaviour (i.e. acting like a textbook private monopolist).

There are reasons to believe this is misleading. In the economic literature on the theory of the public firm, what distinguishes the *public* firm from the *private* firm is the nature of its objective function. Thus, while it is probably reasonable to assume that private firms aim to maximise profits, a public firm or state trading enterprise may pursue different objectives. For example, it could be the case that the state firm aims to maximise social welfare insofar as it takes into account not only its own returns but also the welfare of consumers and/or producers. The implication of this is, of course, that the sales and pricing strategies of a state firm will be different from that of a private firm. Indeed, de Fraja and Delbono (1990) have shown that, in a closed economy, the state firm may set prices equal to those under perfect competition. Thus, in this example, we have a monopolist which pursues objectives, the outcomes of which are identical to a perfectly competitive firm's since the objective function which it has been set is different from the private monopoly case. Thus, it is important to separate institutional form and behaviour.

Distinguishing between the motives of state trading enterprises from private firms is of obvious relevance to the current debate. The WTO notification issue discussed above also highlights the range of objectives state trading enterprises may pursue. These include, among others, "stability in the market", "best possible return from exports", "food security" and so on. Moreover, the reasons for the existence of state involvement in agricultural markets, it has been argued, has been to correct for "distortions" that may arise in agricultural marketing (for example, monopsony power originating at the downstream stage) and to improve returns for farmers by increasing their bargaining power in world as well as domestic markets. As such, state trading enterprises may be perceived as being "welfare enhancing" for the many countries that employ them.

This section has considered the issue of identifying the appropriate benchmark against which to analyse the state trading issue. To summarise: first, it is necessary to separate what the state trading enterprise does from other instruments of a government's agricultural support policy. Second, it is important to define the competitive environment in which state trading enterprises compete. Attempting to measure the trade distorting effect of state trading activities or qualitatively rank state trading enterprises by their likely anti-competitive effect will vary, possibly in a significant manner, when a perfectly competitive benchmark is used rather than allowing for an environment which can be characterised more appropriately as oligopolistic. Third, even though a state trading enterprise may hold a monopoly position, it may nevertheless behave differently from the standard textbook monopoly model. Thus, the possible objectives of the state trading enterprise should also be taken into account. Where a state trading enterprise competes with a small number of private firms, the relevant framework to use is one referred to as "mixed" oligopoly, i.e. where the state trader co-exists and competes with private traders, the main distinction being how their objective functions differ. We consider these issues further in the next sections of this report dealing first with the case of state trading enterprises in importing countries followed by the case of exporting countries.

State trading enterprises in importing countries

Start with the case of an importing country and assume first of all that both the domestic and world markets are competitive and, at least initially, that there is no government intervention in this market in the form of price support or trade policy. In this scenario, the level of imports will be determined by the net difference between domestic supply and demand for the commodity, which can be represented by an import demand schedule. The price for the commodity in this country is equal to the world market price since, by assumption, there is no government policy that affects domestic prices. Suppose now that the government creates a state trading enterprise which is responsible for the sale of the commodity in the domestic economy and the purchase of all imports. In effect this creates a monopoly position for the state trading enterprise which has the potential to influence imports and domestic prices. Assume for the present that the enterprise aims to maximise economic rent by influencing the level of sales in the domestic market.

This outcome is represented in Figure I.1. In the absence of the state trading enterprise, imports were at Q_0 with price P_w, the world market price. With the state trading enterprise, it aims to set marginal revenue equal to marginal cost (P_w) which results in a domestic price equal to P_1, which is in excess of P_w. Apart from the impact on domestic consumers (their welfare declines) and the increase in profits for the state trading enterprise, there is also an impact on the level of trade. At face value, imports have declined from Q_0 to Q_1, i.e. it would appear that market access for foreign exporters owing to the creation of the state trading enterprise has been reduced.

However, one problem with the above scenario is that there is nothing to stop foreign exporters responding to the higher domestic price P_1. Since there is no explicit trade policy instrument to stop imports entering the country, imports will have a pro-competitive effect on the state trading enterprise since imports will expand from Q_1 to Q_0 and return prices to P_w. However, if the government in combination with the creation of the state trading enterprise also puts in place an explicit trade policy instrument, then domestic prices could exceed P_w. If the policy was a tariff on imports, imports still may discipline the state trading enterprise by placing a ceiling on the price that it can charge, unless the tariff was set at suitably high levels.

Alternatively, if the government sets an import quota with imports restricted to Q_1 (with, say, the state trading enterprise managing the import licences), then imports would not be able to have a pro-competitive effect. With the import quota, the demand curve facing the domestic monopolist shifts to ID' (also shown in Figure I.1). This is the residual import demand curve. Since imports cannot increase above the quota level, the domestic monopolist can now set MR' (the marginal revenue curve consistent with the residual import demand curve) equal to Pw with domestic prices now rising towards P_m. At price P_m, the total level of sales in the domestic market are $0Q_m$ plus Q_1Q_0 with Q_0Q_1 being the level of quota-constrained imports.

Figure I.1. Monopoly power in an importing country

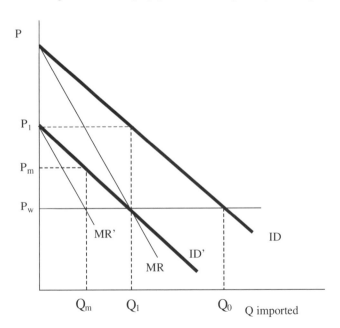

The above discussion makes an important point. State trading enterprises, on their own, may not be able to influence domestic markets in the absence of additional policy instruments. Therefore, when discussing the state trading issue, it is important to separate out the possible sources of domestic market distortions, i.e. those that arise from government policies which will exist irrespective of the presence of the state trading enterprise and those that arise due solely to the latter. For example, it may be the case above that, in the management of the import licences by the state trading enterprise, there is some degree of under-fill of the maximum quota level. However, as the earlier discussion highlighted, there are many possible reasons for quota under-fill and they are not restricted to the presence of state trading enterprises.

The standard analysis outlined above is useful in making the point that the state trading issue should be considered in the context of additional trade policy instruments. However, it has been assumed that the only source of market power arises from the state trading enterprise; the world market is characterised by a large number of sellers and is perfectly competitive. However, as discussed above, there is considerable evidence that, at least for some agricultural markets, this may not be the case. Consequently, the analysis has to be amended to account for the limited number of sellers that may compete with the state trading enterprise in the domestic market. In doing so, we move into the realms of oligopoly theory which is appropriate to highlight the outcome of the interactions of sellers in a given market.

The key issue with oligopoly theory is that the nature of strategic interaction between the players (e.g. the state trading enterprise and the private multinational firms) in the market has to be considered. "Strategic interaction" is important as it attempts to capture how a firm expects its competitors to respond when it pursues its individual objectives. For example, suppose a firm sets prices (or quantities) to maximise its profits. If it is a monopoly, it would not have to bother about how competitors would react to this as there are no other firms in the market, by definition. However, with (a small number of) competitors the firm would have to take into account how it perceives its competitors may respond to its actions. This is the nature of strategic interaction that underlies much of oligopoly theory with economists often confining their assumptions on the nature of strategic interaction to two possibilities. The first assumes the firms choose quantities to maximise profit assuming that the change in their competitor's output choice remains unchanged. The second is where the firm chooses price to maximise profit assuming that its competitor's price choice remains unchanged. The former case is known as a "Cournot game", the latter as a "Bertrand game". In the forthcoming analysis, we restrict ourselves to the former.

Oligopoly theory is essentially mathematical in nature though there are convenient ways to summarise the market outcomes with a limited number of firms and which keeps the essentials of the analysis transparent. This is based on a reaction function approach which highlights the output choice of one firm (or group of firms) in terms of the other. Assuming each firm produces a homogeneous good and their marginal costs are equal, Figure I.2 presents the reaction function framework with two private firms, a domestic firm producing Q_h and a foreign firm producing Q_f. The reaction function for the home firm is R_h, with the reaction function for the foreign firm being given by R_f. Assuming that each firm maximises profits and pursues a Cournot strategy, equilibrium in this market is at C where the reaction functions cross. At this equilibrium, the market is divided equally between the two firms, with the domestic firm supplying Q_h' and the foreign firm Q_f'. Profits for each firm can be represented "iso-profit functions" (not drawn). The important point to note about these profit functions is that profits increase as output for each firm moves along its own output axis.

Of course, there are several variables that can affect the location of this equilibrium. For example, if we increase both the number of foreign and domestic firms, if we allow for product differentiation, and so on, the location of the reaction functions will change. With regard to the change in the number of firms, quantities that are sold in the market will increase and consumer prices will fall. In the limit, as the number of firms increase, the competitive outcome is attained. Moreover, an "asymmetric" outcome may arise. In Figure I.2, we have depicted the "symmetric" case where both firms, with equal marginal costs and producing homogeneous goods, each take 50% of the market and have equal profits. However, a variety of factors can influence the distribution of market shares. For example, differences in marginal costs will change the locations of the reaction functions.

Government policy will also influence the market outcome. Imagine that Figure I.3 represents the case of a domestic market where trade policy is aimed at limiting imports. Initially equilibrium in this market is given by C with each firm supplying Q_f' and Q_h' respectively. If the government imposes a tariff on imports, this shifts RF_f to the left which reduces the level of imports to Q_f" and increases the domestic firm's output to Q_h". Profits for the domestic firm will increase while the foreign firm's profits decline. Given the shape of the reaction functions, domestic prices rise. Alternatively, the government may limit imports with an import quota. Assuming this is set at a level equivalent to the import tariff (in terms of the level of imports that result), this kinks the foreign firm's reaction function (as given by the bold horizontal line) since it cannot expand supply beyond Q_f".

Figure I.2. Market equilibrium with reaction functions

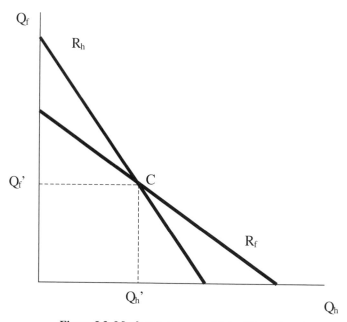

Figure I.3. Market outcomes with tariffs and quotas

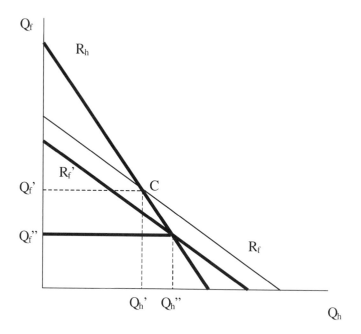

If it was the case that the importing country's market is characterised as a domestic monopoly competing with a single exporting firm, then Figure I.2 and (with the employment of government policies) Figure I.3 could be employed. Note, however, in this analysis, both the foreign and domestic firms are assumed to have the same objective function, i.e. they are both interested in maximising profit. As discussed above, characterising the objective function in this way may not be appropriate for a state trading enterprise which may have a broader set of objectives. If so, the reaction function representing the state trading enterprise's output choice will be different which will result in a different market equilibrium.

Figure I.4 presents the market outcome when a state trading enterprise that does not aim to solely maximise profit competes with a (foreign) private firm that does. We consider two cases. First, the state trading firm aims to maximise its own returns and returns to domestic farmers. This is likely to be broadly in line with the objective function of many state trading enterprises particularly in developed countries. In the second case, the state trading enterprise aims to maximise social welfare, i.e. its own returns, the welfare of domestic farmers and the welfare of domestic consumers. This may be consistent with the objective function of state trading enterprises in developing countries, for example. Equilibrium in this market characterises the outcome with a "mixed" oligopoly.

Initially the private-private equilibrium was at C which is consistent with the equilibrium shown in Figure I.2 above. The other two schedules depict the reaction functions for the state trading enterprise. RF_1 is the state trading enterprise's reaction function when its objective is to maximise its own returns and farmers' welfare. As can be seen, this gives a new equilibrium at D. At this point, the state trading enterprise supplies Q_h'' to the domestic market while the foreign firm's supply has fallen from Q_f' to Q_f''. The flattest schedule represents the state trading enterprise's reaction function when it aims to maximise social welfare. At this point, the foreign firm supplies Q_f''' while the state trading enterprise supplies Q_h'''. Note that if the import quota had been set to be consistent with the initial equilibrium (the horizontal line from Qf' to C in Figure I.4), Q_f'' and Q_f''' would represent quota under-fill. Note also that profit for the foreign firm falls in the above scenario.

What is the intuition behind the above analysis? Consider equilibrium at C. This is the standard duopoly outcome with both firms aiming to maximise profit. If it were appropriate to consider that the state trading enterprise acted as if it were a private firm, then this would be the equilibrium outcome. However, with a different objective function the equilibrium changes. In the case of being concerned with domestic farmers, it is no longer in its interests to sell Q_h' as farmers would not wish to be so constrained on how much they produce. So the state trading enterprise trades off the incentive to maximise profit in the way it would do if it were a private firm with the interests of farmers. The outcome is that — contingent on how it expects the foreign private firm to respond — the optimal choice for the state trading enterprise is to sell more. In other words it acts more competitively by selling more on the domestic market.

Figure I.4. Equilibrium with a state trading enterprise

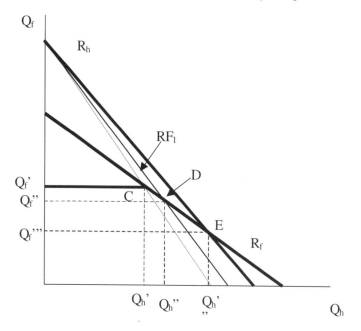

In the case of the state trading enterprise aiming to maximise social welfare, the quantities it is optimal for it to sell on the domestic market are even greater. This is due to the fact that rather than behaving like a private firm which wants to sell at as a high as price as possible, it is also concerned about consumers (as well as farmers). The reason for the higher level of output is that the state trading enterprise sells more so that price is closer to marginal cost, tending towards the outcome that would arise in a competitive market. The higher levels of domestic sales thus reduce sales from the foreign exporter. Given the shape of the reaction functions, consumers clearly benefit as the quantity expansion from the state trading enterprise more than compensates for the decline in imports from the foreign private firm. In line with this, social welfare in the importing country has increased despite the lower level of imports. To the extent to which the state trading enterprise has countered the anti-competitive impact arising from the behaviour of private firms, this improvement in welfare will hold under a broader range of scenarios.

Note also that the new equilibrium has not come about from any explicit government trade instrument (except insofar as the government has sanctioned the existence of the state trading enterprise), unlike the derivation of the new equilibria highlighted in Figure I.3 which was due to the explicit use of tariffs or quotas. Rather, it has been the nature of the state trading enterprise's objective function that has been the source of change. This suggests that it is important to look closely at what state trading enterprises aim to do rather than assuming that they behave like a private monopolist.

Of course, state trading enterprises may also achieve efficiency gains through marketing agricultural output and/or receiving (implicit) subsidies from the government (for example, through access to cheaper credit). This will also affect the market equilibrium and is depicted in Figure I.5. Suppose that the state trading enterprise aimed to maximise its own returns and the welfare of farmers. From the previous discussion, we would expect this to change the shape of the reaction function from that in the profit maximising case. With the efficiency gains (or cheaper credit) this reduces the costs to the state trading enterprise and is represented by a parallel shift in the (flatter) reaction function to R_h''. The new equilibrium is at F which represents a larger market share for the state trading enterprise in its domestic market (Q_h'' instead of Q_h'). Conversely, the foreign exporters' share is reduced (Q_f'' instead of Q_f').

Figure I.5 highlights an important issue. In terms of identifying the impact of state trading enterprises on world markets, it is necessary to consider the reasons why the market equilibrium should change. The move from C to F in Figure I.5 is a combination of effects. Part is due to the nature of the objective function of the state trading enterprise (represented by the dashed reaction function) and part is due to the reduction in its costs (represented by the reaction function R_h'' which is parallel to the dashed reaction function). Clearly, the total move from C to F is not wholly (if at all) due to the anti-competitive practices. Detecting what part of the move from C to F is due to "unfair" competition (for example, by access to cheaper credit) may be a key issue in dealing with state trading enterprises.

The framework employed here is as transparent as possible to highlight the possible impact of a state trading enterprise in an importing country. The analysis could obviously be elaborated (e.g. by increasing the number of foreign firms and so on) but the key points would still stand. It is perhaps useful to summarise these key points.

Figure I.5. State trading enterprise with lower costs

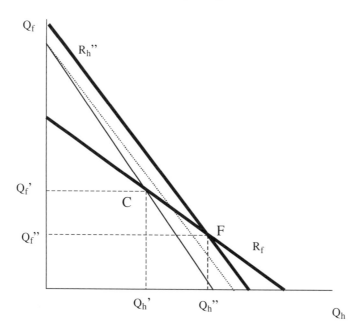

In the case where a state trading enterprise imports from a competitive world market, it is unlikely that the existence of the enterprise alone could distort the domestic market and limit imports. Any market power that the state trading enterprise could exert must also be in conjunction with more explicit trade policy instruments.

When the state trading enterprise competes with a limited number of private firms, the nature of competition between these firms has to be taken into account. Again, the use of explicit trade policy instruments can affect competition between the limited number of participants in this market.

When considering the impact of a state trading enterprise it is important to distinguish between form and the objectives. While it may appear at face value that the state trading enterprise may be monopolist (insofar as there is only one of them), nevertheless its objective function may cause it to behave more competitively than a private monopolist.

The implications for the foreign suppliers in terms of market access will depend on the nature of this objective function. In the two cases examined, imports decline and, if an import quota had been in place, it might not have been filled. However, this under-fill is not due to problems related to the allocation of import licences.

Note also that the lower level of market access is consistent with a relatively more competitive domestic market (in terms of total quantities sold) and lower prices for consumers, if the state trading enterprise is assumed to have the objective of maximising consumer welfare along with producer welfare and profits.

In terms of the combination of effects that the state trading enterprise may have on foreign firms' access to domestic markets, efficiency gains or access to cheap credit also may be important. However, it is important to separate the 'total' change into the possible combination of effects taking into account the nature of the state trading enterprise's objective function.

State trading enterprises in exporting countries

State trading enterprises also exist among exporting countries. In many respects, the issues that have been considered in our discussion of state trading enterprises in importing countries also arise here. In other words, it is important to consider the role of government policies, identify the number of competitors against which the state trading enterprise competes, how to characterise their interaction and the nature of the state trading enterprise's objective function. As such, the framework we have introduced above could be used here. However, there are some further considerations that we should deal with in the exporter case. Specifically, depending on the type of commodity, is domestic consumption important and, if it is, does the state trading enterprise have exclusive rights to sell in the domestic market as well as being responsible for exports (i.e. does it have 'single-desk' status)?

We start with the case where there is no domestic consumption and where the country is a monopoly supplier to the competitive export market of the good in question. This is the standard case of a monopoly exporter well-known from trade theory and is represented in Figure I.6. The EX curve represents the demand for this country's exports with MR_x being the marginal revenue curve consistent with this schedule. The equilibrium outcome in this case is for the monopoly exporter to equalise marginal revenue with marginal cost, supply Q_1 rather than Q_0 to the world market, resulting in a price for its exports equal to P_x which is in excess of P_w. In this case, the monopoly supplier enjoys a positive level of economic rent (or abnormal profit). Note also in this case that the successful exertion of market power is not dependent on the existence of an explicit trade policy instrument as in the importing country case

(Figure I.1). Note also that since there is no domestic consumption, only foreign consumers are exploited and domestic welfare has increased. If there were a larger number of suppliers from this country, the trade policy instrument that would have an equivalent effect would be an optimal export tax set at $(P_x - P_w)$.

Figure I.6. A monopoly export supplier: no domestic consumption

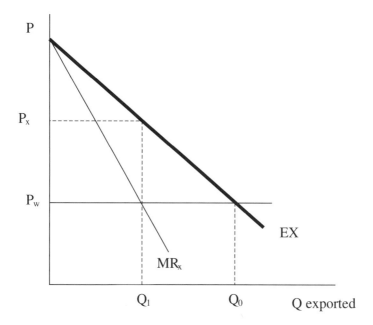

If imperfect competition exists in world agricultural markets, it is likely to be characterised by competition among a small number of exporters rather than only one. Indeed, most of the academic studies on competition in the world grains market for instance highlight the interaction between a small number of participants. Consequently, the reaction function framework can be used again though this time the 'market space' relates to the world market for the commodity in question. As before, it is assumed that market participants maximise their objective functions by choosing the quantities to sell on the world market and assume Cournot behaviour with respect to their competitors. The commodity sold is homogeneous and marginal costs for each supplier are constant and equal. In this example, again we assume that there is no domestic consumption.

Figure I.7 characterises equilibrium in this scenario. Initially assume that each participant in the market aims to maximise profit. R_h therefore represents the home reaction function and R_f the foreign reaction function with

39

the equilibrium being given where the reaction functions cross (at point E). At this point, the world market is divided equally between the two suppliers with the home country supplying Q_h' and the foreign country, Q_f'. As before, the equilibrium here is characterised as being symmetric; however, a range of factors can cause market shares to be divided unevenly between the home and foreign suppliers. One possibility is the use of export subsidies; if the foreign government paid an export subsidy to its supplier, this would shift R_f (to R_f') to the right, thus giving the foreign supplier a higher market share (Q_f' to Q_f") and the home supplier a lower market share (Q_h' to Q_h"). The new equilibrium at E' would be consistent with an increase in profits for the foreign supplier while profits for the domestic supplier would decline.

Figure I.7. Competition in world export markets

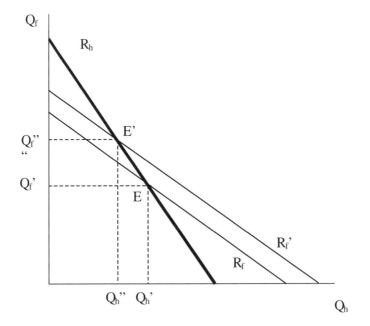

Now consider the case where the supply of the home country's exports is the responsibility of a state trading enterprise. If the objective function of the state trading enterprise was to maximise profit, it would be indistinguishable from a private firm and equilibrium in the export market would be exactly the same as that given in Figure I.7 (i.e. in the absence of any government policies, at point E). However, as we now know, this may be an inappropriate characterisation of a state trading enterprise's activities. Suppose in this case the state trading enterprise aims to maximise its own returns and domestic farmers'

welfare. (It would be uninterested in consumer welfare as we have assumed no domestic consumption). The outcome is shown in Figure I.8. The state trading enterprise's reaction function is now flatter, resulting in a new equilibrium at E'. At E', the home country's share of the world export market has now increased (Q_h' to Q_h") at the expense of exports from the foreign country (Q_f' to Q_f").

There are several points to note about this new equilibrium. First, market shares have changed even though no explicit trade policy instrument (such as an export subsidy) has been used. The equilibrium is due solely to considering an alternative objective function for the state trading enterprise. Second, the intuition for this new equilibrium is that the state trading enterprise supplies more to the world export market because it is concerned with farmers' welfare not just the maximum level of profit it can attain for itself. Third, note that the new equilibrium would also be consistent with a private firm having the benefit of an export subsidy. The objective function of the state trading enterprise causes the shape of its reaction function to change — it becomes flatter, thus giving the new equilibrium at E'. However, the same outcome could have been attained by a parallel shift in R_h to pass-through point E' (as given by the 'broken' reaction function). This parallel shift would have been induced by a corresponding export subsidy.

Figure I.8. State trading enterprises in an oligopolistic export market

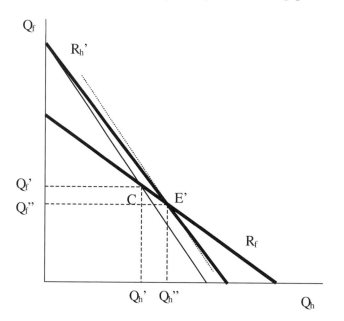

As discussed in the case of the importing country, we should also consider other effects associated with the state trading enterprise, for example, the potential efficiency gains due to having a single marketing board rather than a large number of small sellers and the case of (implicit) subsidies [Markusen (1984) and Rodrik (1989)]. However, the analysis would be similar to that reported above and is not repeated here.

Now consider the case where the state trading enterprise is responsible for selling the commodity in the domestic market as well as for exporting the commodity, i.e. unlike the previous example, we have to take account of domestic consumption. Assume that in the domestic market, the state trading enterprise has exclusive rights such that the domestic market can be characterised as a monopoly. However, although the state trading enterprise has exclusive rights to sell on world markets, it nevertheless competes with (a limited number) of other firms such that the world market is more competitive than the domestic market, albeit still oligopolistic. What would be the appropriate strategy for the state trading enterprise in this case?

Figure I.9. Export markets with domestic consumption

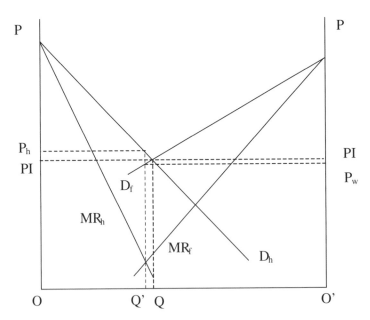

Figure I.9 characterises this scenario. There are two demand schedules, D_h representing the demand schedule in the domestic market and D_f the demand schedule in the world market. D_f is flatter than D_h which represents the fact that demand in the world market is more elastic (due, for example, to the number of substitutes available from other sources). The quantities sold by the state trading enterprise can be identified from the horizontal axis and the prices charged in the domestic and world markets from the relevant vertical axes. If the domestic and world markets were "integrated", i.e. they were regarded by the state trading enterprise as a single, unified market, the state trading enterprise would charge the same price in each market. This outcome is given where the two demand schedules cross, with the price being charged in each market being equal to PI and the quantities sold in the domestic and world market being OQ and O'Q respectively.

However, this is not an optimal strategy for the state trading enterprise. If markets are "segmented", i.e. arbitrage between the two markets can be prevented, the optimal strategy for the state trading enterprise, if the aim is to maximise profit, is to charge different prices in each market. Specifically, the state trading enterprise will equalise marginal revenue from each market. This is given where the two marginal revenue functions cross. MR_f is the marginal revenue function corresponding to D_f and MR_h is the marginal revenue function corresponding to D_h. Where these two schedules cross determines how much is sold in each market. From Figure I.9, it is apparent that OQ' is sold in the domestic market and O'Q' is sold in the world market. Compared with the "integrated market" case, sales to domestic consumers are restricted while, at the same, time, exports to the world market have increased. Consequently, the price that domestic consumers have to pay rises to P_h while the price for the good on world markets falls to P_w. This is essentially the outcome that arises from "single desk" status with producers being paid a weighted average of the two prices.

Figure I.9 shows that it is optimal for the state trading enterprise to charge different prices in different markets. By doing so, it is maximising its objective function, i.e. maximising returns. However, in this case, the state trading enterprise may be accused of practising price discrimination or even dumping. While for many competitors this may seem like an abuse of market power, insofar as the state trading enterprise expands its share of world markets and reduces the profits of its competitors, nevertheless price discrimination by state trading enterprises is not necessarily prohibited under GATT. As a note to Article XVII states:

"The charging by a state enterprise of different prices for its sale of a product is not precluded by the provisions of this Article, provided that such different prices are charged for commercial reasons, to meet conditions of supply and demand in export markets." (WTO 1995a, p. 550, Ad Article XVII:1)

Clearly, whether the outcome of charging different prices in different markets as shown in Figure I.9 is adjudged to be anti-competitive or not will likely depend on the interpretation of "commercial reasons".

As before, the outcome as characterised arises without any explicit government policies bar the approval of establishing a state trading enterprise in the first place. However, as in the previous examples, the behaviour of the state trading enterprise is equivalent to the use of explicit trade instruments. For example, the outcome in Figure I.9 could have arisen in the context where there is no state trading enterprise and no market power. For example, if the government paid an export subsidy to exporters, more would be sold on the world market and, with some constraints on supply, less sold in the domestic market. By the increase in sales to world markets, world prices would fall while domestic prices rise, assuming that some degree of market segmentation exists. Note in passing the contrast between the cases with and without domestic consumption.

In many countries, the process of regulatory reform and privatisation has permitted private firms to compete with the state trading enterprises. In the context of the current example, this could be characterised by private firms also being allowed to sell the good in the domestic market. In the terminology of the framework used here, there is a "mixed" oligopoly in the domestic market and a "mixed" oligopoly in the world market. How does the increase in competition in the domestic market affect the outcome shown in Figure I.9? Essentially, the ability of the state trading enterprise to raise domestic prices becomes more limited. Since the state trading enterprise will no longer have control of domestic supply, its ability to raise domestic prices will be limited. In the context of Figure I.9, the MR_h curve will be flatter, which leads to lower prices in the home market and a reduction in exports to the world market. Consequently, the extent of price discrimination will be reduced.

There are two further issues worthy of consideration in this conceptual analysis. First, the nature of competition that has been depicted in the above examples has related to a state trading enterprise competing with private firms. What separates these two forms of market participants from a conceptual point of view is the how their objective functions vary. However, given the prevalence of state trading enterprises in world agricultural trade, it may be more relevant to characterise competition, at least in certain markets, as being one where state trading enterprises compete with each other. How will the outcome vary in this case?

The answer will depend on how the objective functions differ between the two state trading enterprises (as well as other attributes arising from the existence of the state trading enterprise, e.g. efficiency gains or access to cheaper credit, or other government policies). Assume, for example, that both state trading enterprises aim to maximise "joint returns", i.e. their own export revenue and the welfare of their domestic farmers. The outcome is characterised in Figure I.10. Point C characterises the outcome if the private traders aim solely to maximise profit. This is the standard Cournot outcome. However, with the state trading enterprises in each country having different objectives, the slopes of both reaction functions change. The new equilibrium is given at point S with the home country's state trading enterprise selling Q_h'' (instead of Q_h') and the foreign state trading enterprise selling Q_f'' (instead of Q_f'). Since total quantities sold on the world market have increased, world prices fall. Note that the world market is now more competitive even though the number of market participants has not increased. This outcome underlines the importance that it is not just numbers that matter but how these enterprises compete on the world market.

A second point to consider is where a state trading enterprise not only competes directly with a limited number of private traders but also sells to a limited number of buyers that dominate the downstream stage. For example, in motivating their criticisms of the current debate on the state trading issue, Veeman *et al.* (*op. cit.*) note that this characterisation is appropriate for much of the world grain trade. We can think intuitively as to what may happen. If the downstream stage is oligopolistic, this reduces the quantities sold in the downstream market. Since how much is sold in the downstream market determines the derived demand for the output of upstream firms/state trading enterprises, it is clear that the nature of competition at the downstream stage determines the market outcome in the upstream stage. Hence, it is not only the nature of competition among direct competitors that matters but also the nature of competition throughout the whole agricultural/food marketing system. In the context of the framework we have been using in this report, the appropriate characterisation is a model of "successive oligopoly" as opposed to "single stage oligopoly". Essentially, the market equilibrium in all of the figures above will change because the nature of downstream competition will change the "derived" marginal revenue function and change the shape of the relevant reaction functions.

Figure I.10. Competition between state trading enterprises

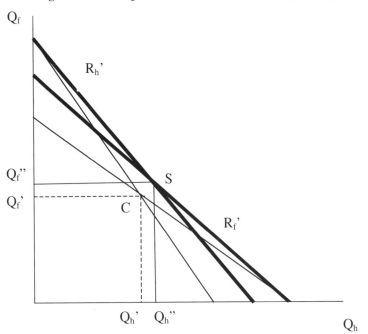

The framework used here to evaluate the effects on competition in the world export market of state trading enterprises yields a few key points. These include:

- In the case where a state trading enterprise competes with a private firm, the outcome is altered depending on the shape of the state trading enterprise's objective function. Unlike the importer case, the changed outcome is not dependent on an explicit policy.

- When an exporting state trading enterprise also has a monopoly on domestic sales, the possibility for price segmentation means that a higher price will be charged domestically than internationally, leaving the possibility of accusations of dumping.

- In both of these cases, the results stemming from the difference between the objective functions of a state trading enterprise and a private firm are consistent with the results obtained from the use of government policy, such as an export subsidy, with a private firm.

- Different results are also obtained depending on the nature of the competitors faced by a state trading enterprise. In the case of two state enterprises competing in the world export market, the results are more competitive than with a private oligopoly.

- The nature of competition throughout the system also has an effect on outcomes. Competition in downstream industries will determine the quantities and prices in upstream industries.

Assessment of specific concerns

There are a variety of concerns about the trade effects of state trading enterprises. These concerns are reported in a number of sources, including Ackerman (1998), Veeman *et al.* (1999), Dixit and Josling (1997), Ingco and Ng (1998). While the section above highlighted a few of the more important ones, this section gives a detailed list and an initial assessment of the issues. They have been broken down into those relating to state trading enterprises in general, those relating to importing state trading enterprises, and those relating to exporting state trading enterprises. In this section, an attempt is made to evaluate which issues are specific to state trading enterprises, as opposed to which are general competition issues. We will further assess whether the concerns are dealt with in the GATT/WTO legal texts, whether the model and theoretical framework proposed below can shed some light, and whether empirical research is needed.

Concerns in general

Concern 1: State trading enterprises distort trade relative to the competitive market solution.

Comment: The competitive market solution is probably not the relevant benchmark against which to compare the *status quo*. Given the prevalence of a few multinational companies that deal with commodities, some form of imperfect competition would be more relevant. This contention is supported by empirical evidence, at least for the international wheat market. The empirical issue is to determine which form is most relevant on a case-by-case basis and to assess the significance of the distortion.

Concern 2: State trading enterprises will use their powers to circumvent their URAA commitments on market access, domestic support and export subsidies.

Comment: While it is possible that state trading enterprises may behave in this way, the hypothetical possibility needs to be carefully investigated empirically. The notification and counter-notifications to the Committee on Trade in Goods is one way to make progress and to determine whether, in specific circumstances, the concern is justified.

Concern 3: The fundamental concern is that state trading enterprises are in a position to undermine competitive market norms and distort international agricultural trade because of their position.

Comment: This concern appears to ignore the constraints placed on state trading enterprises in general by the many Articles of the GATT. The Articles, including Article XVII, recognise that state trading enterprises must conform to commercial practice, otherwise they will distort trade, albeit perhaps not from the competitive norm. This has been a long-standing concern about state trading enterprises in general, which is why they are referred to in several Articles (WTO 1997, p. 58).

Concern 4: State trading enterprises that are given monopoly/monopsony rights can pool prices and distort competition.

Comment: This is a legitimate concern because there is nothing in the Articles applying to or referring to state trading enterprises that can prevent price pooling, except Article XVI. An exception is, however, made for subsidies applied to primary agricultural products. The model proposed above does not explicitly address the issue of price pooling.

Concern 5: It is not obvious what the objective function of a state trading enterprise is.

Comment: To the extent that state trading enterprises are not profit maximisers, and the evidence from the notifications to the WTO outlined above suggests that in most cases they are not, one has to consider closely what the impact of a state trading enterprise is likely to be. As will be shown by the model, their choice of objective function is important.

Concern 6: State trading enterprises can limit the quantities of exports or they can limit the volumes of imports in contravention of Article XI.

Comment: If it is found that a state trading enterprise is in breach of Article XI on the import side, then the Dispute Settlement process is available. It has been shown above that an importing state trading enterprise cannot on its own limit imports. A trade policy must also be present. However, there is nothing in the GATT to prevent a country restricting exports if done in a way consistent with Article XI(1). Indeed, in the mid-1990s, when the EU restricted exports of grains by imposing an export tax, an STE was not involved and the action was consistent with that Article. It is unlikely, given the structure of international commodity markets and a probable price elastic demand, that a state trading enterprise would restrict exports to particular markets. Such a strategy would not be rational.

Concerns about exporting state trading enterprises

The following concerns have been expressed about the hypothetical behaviour of exporting state trading enterprises. However, the empirical evidence remains elusive.

Concern 1: State trading enterprises can circumvent the export subsidy commitments of the URAA:

- as monopsonists, they can lower the prices offered to producers;

- as monopolists, they can charge consumers higher prices; and

- taken together, this means that additional revenues can be generated to subsidise exports when the state trading enterprise is a monopoly exporter.

Comment: In the absence of assumptions about the nature of domestic competition regulations and agricultural price intervention by central government, there is nothing to prevent a private firm from behaving in just the same way as a state trading enterprise. Therefore, this is a concern about imperfect competition as much as about the effects of exclusive rights accorded a state trading enterprise.

Concern 2: State trading enterprises (with monopsony powers) have greater security of supply and, therefore, it is easier for them than it is for private firms to make long-term commitments with importing country governments.

Comment: This argument rests on the notion that importing countries with a state trading enterprise in place use a model of portfolio diversification amongst exporters in order to reduce price and quantity risk in their decisions about import sources. There is some evidence (Carter, 1992) that this may occur.

Concern 3: State trading enterprises can receive price underwriting that:

- reduces their exposure to price risk;

- allows them to borrow at reduced interest rates; and

- together, enables them to offer lower prices to foreign buyers.

Comment: For agricultural products, price underwriting is a form of subsidy and, therefore, is legal under Article XVI as well as the Agreement on Agriculture. If the real issue is the provision of a subsidy rather than the nature of the entity receiving it, then agriculture should be brought into line with other goods. Nevertheless, as was shown in Section 8, such subsidies will increase exports and market share. However, there is also evidence (Carter, Loyns and Berwald, 1998) that state trading enterprises may over service their exports and this would tend to increase prices somewhat and offset at least part of the implicit subsidy.

Concern 4: State trading enterprises can benefit from various tax breaks, transport subsidies, and favourable foreign exchange rates, all of which enable them to offer lower prices in export markets.

Comment: All of these arrangements could be given to private firms. Again, it is the assistance provided rather than the nature of the receiver that is of concern.

Concern 5: There is a lack of transparency in the pricing practices of state trading enterprises.

Comment: Pricing issues are also important in private firms in which pricing practices are unlikely to be revealed under imperfect competition because of the commercial sensitivities induced by the nature of their strategic interaction.

Concern 6: State trading enterprises may indulge in practices unavailable to private companies that are not offered the special rights enjoyed by state trading enterprises, for example:

- marketing contracts; and

- price pooling.

Comment: Private firms have opportunities to provide marketing contracts. As well, a private monopolist would be able to pool prices. The concern is one of domestic competition policy and market contestability.

Concern 7: State trading enterprises affect world market prices if they have market power in the world market.

Comment: This is a concern not about ownership of the firm but about market power *per se* and is equally applicable to private firms. If the product is differentiated, then even a market structure that supports a large number of firms (monopolist competition) would reveal that individual firms had market power because the demand function facing them was downward sloping. Moreover, there may not be a single world market, but rather a set of segmented markets within which some firms compete but others do not.

Concerns about importing state trading enterprises

Concern 1: State trading enterprises may regulate domestic demand in ways that are different from the effects of a tariff.

Comment: In the post-Uruguay Round world of no non-tariff barriers on imports of agricultural products (with the exception of TRQs in some countries and for some products), this is an important concern. Nevertheless, state trading enterprises are bound by Article II:4 and Article XVII:4(b) to restrict their mark-ups on imports so as to produce the same effects on the volume of imports as would the bound tariff rate.

Concern 2: State trading enterprises may not be basing their pricing on "commercial considerations", but, instead, they could be discriminating amongst exporters.

Comment: Such behaviour would be in breach of Articles I and XVII:1 and would be subject in the normal way to a Dispute Settlement resolution.

Concern 3: State trading enterprises that are set up to administer TRQs could stifle domestic competition.

Comment: Domestic competition is determined by the nature of domestic competition law. It is not obvious how a state trading enterprise, in the absence of much more detail on competition policy, could be accused of stifling domestic competition unless it prevented downstream firms from gaining access to the imported product. Moreover, since the fill rates of TRQs controlled by state trading enterprises has been amongst the highest of the fill rates of the ten or so methods used, the evidence of stifling competition is not strong.

Concern 4: State trading enterprises can control grades and standards.

Comment: It is not obvious what the nature of this concern is as direct government regulations can also control grades and standards, in the absence of a state trading enterprise. It is more likely that the grades and standards are set by government and implemented through the state trading enterprise. Therefore, the problem is one of government policy rather than the state trading enterprise *per se*.

Concern 5: State trading enterprises can benefit by controlling multiple exchange rates.

Comment: Again, the benefits of multiple exchange rates could be gained by private firms, if the multiplicity is attached by government to imports of specific goods.

Concern 6: The special privileges given state trading enterprises are not consistent with domestic competition policy.

Comment: This concern is certainly real. If it is to carry weight, however, then the nature of domestic competition policy needs to be elaborated. Within countries, governments often apply lax rules to firms trading internationally while applying stricter rules to those operating domestically.

Concern 7: Some state trading enterprises control the domestic market as well as imports, so distorting resource allocation.

Comment: Distorting domestic resource allocation is really not a trade issue unless these distortions cause trade distortions. It is unclear why state trading enterprises should be the concern here when governments have pursued, and continue to pursue, various alternative policy instruments which distort import volumes and prices, as well as domestic production or consumption decisions.

Concern 8: Monopsony state trading enterprises break the link between domestic consumer prices and international prices.

Comment: This argument is now more important than it was pre-URAA because all non-tariff barriers have this same effect. If the argument is basically about price transmission from the international market to the domestic market, then this is a concern.

Concern 9: State trading enterprises can mark-up in excess of bound tariff rates.

Comment: Such behaviour would be in contravention of Article II:4 and the Dispute Settlement process could be followed.

Concern 10: State trading enterprises can contravene national treatment (Article III).

Comment: This would seem to be a general concern about the potential activities of a state trading enterprise and not one peculiar to those in agriculture. The usual redress is possible.

Concern 11: State trading enterprises can engage in cross-subsidisation and distort market signals.

Comment: This concern is based upon the notion of perfect competition. In imperfect competition, it would be possible for private firms to engage in such practices, not only within a country but also between countries through transfer pricing.

Concern 12: State trading enterprises can limit market access and protect domestic producers from international competition.

Comment: Again, this seems a much more general concern than one purely dependent upon a state trading enterprise as a trade barrier. Any policy instrument that impedes imports achieves an identical outcome. Yet, there is little clamour to remove all barriers to international trade in agricultural products and, hence, this concern about state trading enterprises can carry no weight. Moreover, as will be shown, in the absence of a specific trade policy instrument the state trading enterprise faces the world price and, therefore, cannot protect domestic producers through raising prices or by restricting imports.

Conclusions

The issue of the role and impact of state trading enterprises may be high on the forthcoming agenda in the WTO on liberalising agricultural trade. We have outlined the status of state trading enterprises in the GATT/WTO, reviewed the concerns that have been raised in relation to the ways in which state trading enterprises may affect market access and competition on world agricultural markets, and outlined the proposals that have recently been offered as a means to deal with the state trading "issue" in the WTO negotiations.

On the whole, there has been limited research on the impact that state trading enterprises may have on world agricultural trade. The existing literature on the state trading issue (which has been reflected in the recent proposals dealing with state trading) assumes that state enterprises have market power (due to the nature of their "exclusive rights and special privileges") yet that they compete in otherwise competitive markets. Recently, this market environment in which state trading enterprises compete has been disputed (Veeman *et al.*, 1999) as well as existing academic research on this issue). To the extent that state trading enterprises compete in oligopolistic markets this may change the way in which policy-makers should think about the state trading issue. At the very least, the impact of state trading enterprises' activities will be quantitatively different when compared with a more competitive market environment.

The aim was to present a conceptual framework that would characterise state trading enterprises competing in oligopolistic markets, i.e. with a limited number of private firms or other state trading enterprises. Both the importing and exporting country cases were considered. From this conceptual analysis, we established several key points that should be taken into account when considering the state trading issue. These can be summarised as follows:

- It is important to separate the actions of state trading enterprises from general government policy towards its domestic agricultural sector and agricultural trade policy. Particularly in the import case, the potential market power of the state trading enterprise may only be possible in conjunction with the government's use of explicit trade policy instruments. Thus, despite the fears of some commentators, the benefits from trade liberalisation may still be felt even in the continued presence of state trading enterprises. Changing the rules for explicit trade policy instruments may, in some cases, act to circumscribe the potential market power of state trading enterprises.

- If it is appropriate to characterise state trading enterprises competing with a limited number of private firms (or with each other), then the framework should be one that accounts for imperfect competition rather than perfect competition. This makes the analysis more relevant though arguably more complicated and often dependent on the assumptions of the particular model used. This is especially relevant if research is aimed at empirically assessing the impact of state trading enterprises in oligopolistic markets. In terms of the current debate, it is important that policy-makers and trade negotiators consider what the appropriate "benchmark" is and how that benchmark would change even if all state trading enterprises were prohibited.

- From the conceptual framework used, it was emphasised that policy makers should clearly distinguish between the monopoly aspect of a state trading enterprise and the nature of its objective function. Much of the current debate effectively assumes that a state trading enterprise behaves in the same manner as a private firm that enjoys a monopoly position. However, it could be argued that the public nature of the state trading enterprise distinguishes it from a private firm. This is important in terms of assessing the impact of state trading enterprises on agricultural trade since, although a state trading enterprise may hold a monopoly position, it may not behave in a traditional textbook manner. Indeed the nature of a state trading enterprise's objective function may lead to an outcome that is more competitive than the private oligopoly case as many of the examples in the text have shown. In this case, the appropriate benchmark to refer to relates to a "mixed" oligopoly.

- Another way to think about this issue is to consider what differentiates a state trading enterprise from a private firm. To take a slightly different example, state trading enterprises are often accused of having monopsony power due to their "exclusive" status. But how, in the absence of any government policy, would this differ from a private firm which also maintained a monopoly? By being a single seller, it is likely to also be a single purchaser. If state trading enterprises were to be prohibited following WTO negotiations, to be effective in promoting trade liberalisation, some thought should be given to the nature of the market structure which would replace it.

- Of course, there may be other aspects of trade featuring state trading enterprises that are not captured solely by differences in the objective function. Efficiency gains may arise through the use of a single marketing agency (which experiences increasing returns to scale) and this can affect the market outcome. Similarly, access to cheaper credit or other implicit subsidies will also be important. The problem then involves separating the range of effects due to the state trading enterprise and determining what is acceptable in terms of how it may affect other countries and what is not. For example, a state trading enterprise that reduces the costs of marketing and, by doing so, increases its market share may be regarded as an acceptable "commercial practice". However, a state trading enterprise that has access to cheaper credit from the central government may not, even though both may have similar impacts on export competition or domestic market access. The problem relates to distinguishing between the two.

There is clearly much scope and need for further research if the issue of state trading enterprises is to be fully and appropriately addressed in the WTO round of negotiations. Information on state trading enterprises is a necessary first step. In order to evaluate state trading enterprises, it is important to have precise and detailed knowledge of how the various state trading enterprises are organised, along with their role in domestic and international markets. Using that information, a number of avenues can be explored. Here, we highlight two of the most obvious.

First, it should be recognised that state trading enterprises are heterogeneous in nature insofar as the objectives of a state trading enterprise may vary from country to country. In our framework, we considered two alternative objectives that a state trading enterprise may pursue. One possibility was that the state trading enterprise was concerned with its own returns and the welfare of the domestic farmers it represents. The other was that the state trading enterprise was, in addition, concerned with consumer welfare. Of course, there are likely to be many variants of these two objectives that could be considered (food security, etc.). The key point is that the nature of this objective function is important in assessing the impact of the state trading enterprise on other market participants.

A second priority for research should be to attempt to assess the impact of state trading enterprises on world export markets and in relation to domestic market access. Using empirical oligopoly models is in many ways more difficult than perfectly competitive models, but there is nevertheless a growing range of tools with which to make this type of assessment. Although data requirements may be constraining and the analysis limited to specific markets, it may be useful nevertheless to develop a quantitative approach that could accompany more formal analysis in an attempt to gauge how important the state trading issue really is.

Overall, the key conclusion is the need for careful empirical work on both the practices and the effects of state trading enterprises. The framework developed demonstrates the importance of considering the actual effects of state trading enterprises rather than the potential effects. While the theoretical model points out those issues that are important in terms of potential effects, empirical research is needed to assess whether the potential impacts are translated into actual effects in the world trading system. Furthermore, any empirical evidence regarding the circumvention of GATT rules by state trading enterprises also needs to be carefully examined.

NOTES

1.   Report prepared for OECD by Steve McCorriston (University of Exeter, United Kingdom) and Donald MacLaren (University of Melbourne, Australia), October 1999.

2.   This interest by the U.S. in state trading enterprises pre-dates the implementation of the URAA. During the Uruguay Round, the U.S. supported Chile in its proposal to the Negotiating Group on GATT Articles that Article XVII be evaluated (Croome 1995, p. 97). This proposal was not adopted by the Group.

3.   Farmers in Canada determine how much to deliver to the CWB taking into account other marketing opportunities such as off-board sales as feed grains or non-food uses. After harvest, farmers arrange delivery contracts with the CWB. In the period 1994-95/1998-99, the CWB accounted for 77% of domestic procurement. In Australia, the AWB accounted for 86% of domestic procurement according to WTO notifications.

4.   Information presented in Part II, is an attempt to organise this sort of information around objective criteria, while avoiding subjective judgements. For example, these criteria include such items as the level of control of imports and exports, the types of trade policy instruments in place, product range and transparency, and ownership and relationship with government.

5.   This type of analysis is currently undertaken by the OECD using the Producer and Consumer Support Estimates (PSE/CSE) and the Policy Evaluation Matrix (PEM). The PSE and CSE estimate the level of government support for agriculture, regardless of where this support originates, while the PEM is being developed in order to consider the impact of this support on various aspects of the economy. Information on support using the PSE and CSE is available in the annual OECD report, *Agricultural Policies in OECD Countries: Monitoring and Evaluation* (OECD 1999).

BIBLIOGRAPHY

ABARE (1999), *WTO Agricultural Negotiations: Important Market Access Issues*, Research Report 99.3, Canberra, Australia.

Abbott, P.C. and P.K.S. Kallio (1996), "Implications of Game Theory for International Agricultural Trade", *American Journal of Agricultural Economics*, N°78, pp. 738-744.

Ackerman, K. (1997), "State Trading Enterprises: Their Role in World Markets", *Agricultural Outlook*, June, USDA.

Ackerman, K. (1998) "State Trading Enterprises in World Agricultural Trade", *Agriculture in the WTO*, USDA, ERS, WRS-98-4, December.

Ackerman, K. and P. Dixit (1998), *An Overview of the Extent of State Trading in World Agricultural Markets*, mimeo, USDA.

Alouze, C.M., A.S. Watson and N.H. Sturgess (1978), "Oligopoly Pricing in the World Wheat Market", *American Journal of Agricultural Economics*, N°60, pp. 173-185.

Carter, C. A. (1992), "The Participation of China and the Soviet Union in the Global Wheat Market" Chapter 4 in T. Becker, R. Gray and A. Schmitz (eds.), *Improving Agricultural Trade Performance under the GATT*, Wissenschaftsverlag, Vauk, Kiel.

Carter, C.A., R.M.A. Loyns and D.Berwald (1998), "Domestic Costs of Statutory Marketing Authorities: The Case of the Canadian Wheat Board", *American Journal of Agricultural Economics*, N°80, pp. 313-324.

Croome, J. (1995) *Reshaping the World Trading System: A history of the Uruguay Round*, World Trade Organisation, Geneva.

Davey, W. J. (1998) "Article XVII GATT: An Overview", in T. Cottier and P.C. Mavriodis (eds.), *State Trading in the 21st Century*, Michigan University Press, Michigan.

De Fraja, G. and F. Delbono (1990), "Game Theoretic Models of Mixed Oligopoly", *Journal of Economic Surveys*, N°4, pp. 1-17.

Dixit, P. and T. Josling (1997) *State Trading in Agriculture: An Analytical Framework*, International Agricultural Trade Research Consortium Working Paper 97-4, University of Minnesota.

Ingco, M. and F. Ng (1998) *Distortionary Effects of State Trading in Agriculture: Issues for the Next Round of Multilateral Trade Negotiations*, World Bank, Washington D.C.

Karp L.S. and A.F. McCalla (1983) "Dynamic games and international trade: an application to the world corn market", *American Journal of Agricultural Economics*, N°65, pp 641-656.

Kolstad, C.D. and A.E. Burris (1986) "Imperfectly competitive equilibria in international commodity markets", *American Journal of Agricultural Economics*, N°68, pp. 27-36.

Lloyd, P.J. (1982) 'State Trading and the Theory of International Trade" in M.M. Kostecki (ed.) *State Trading in International Markets*, St. Martin's Press, New York.

Markusen, J. R. (1984) "The Welfare and Allocative Effects of Export Taxes versus Marketing Boards", *Journal of Development Economics*, N°14, pp. 19-36.

McCalla, A.F. (1966) "A Duopoly Model of World Wheat Pricing", *American Journal of Agricultural Economics*, N°48, pp. 711-727.

McCalla, A.F. and A. Schmitz (1982) "State Trading in Agriculture" in M.M. Kostecki (ed.), *State Trading in International Markets*, St. Martin's Press, New York.

OECD (1999), *Agricultural Policies in OECD Countries, Volume 1: Monitoring and Evaluation*, OECD, Paris.

Pick, D. H. and T.A. Park (1991), "The Competitive Structure of U.S. Agricultural Exports", *American Journal of Agricultural Economics*, N°73, pp. 133-141.

Pick, D. H. and C.A. Carter (1994), 'Pricing to Market with Transactions Denominated in a Common Currency', *American Journal of Agricultural Economics*, N°76, pp. 55-60.

Rodrik, D. (1989) "Trade Taxes for a Large Country with Non-Atomistic Firms", *Journal of International Economics*, N°26 (1/2), pp. 157-167.

Schmitz, J. (1996), *The Role Played by Public Enterprises: How Much Does It Differ Across Countries?*, Federal Reserve Bank of Minneapolis Quarterly Review, N°20, pp. 2-15.

UNCTAD (1990), *Handbook of State Trading Organisations*, UNCTAD, Geneva.

Veeman, M., M. Fulton and B. Larue (1999), *International Trade in Agricultural and Food Products: The Role of State Trading Enterprises*, Report for Agriculture and Agri-Food Canada.

WTO (1995*a*), *The Results of the Uruguay Round of Multilateral Trade Negotiations: The Legal Texts*, Geneva.

WTO (1995*b*) *Operations of State Trading Enterprises as they relate to International Trade*, G/STR/2, Geneva.

WTO (1997), *Annual Report Volume I, Special Topic: Trade and Competition Policy*, Geneva.

Young, L. and P.C. Abbott (1998),*Wheat Importing State Trading Enterprises: Impacts on the World Wheat Market*, paper presented at the AAEA Annual Meeting, Salt Lake City, United States.

PART II.

A REVIEW OF STATE TRADING ENTERPRISES IN AGRICULTURE IN oecd MEMBER COUNTRIES

Introduction

Many studies have been undertaken on state trading and/or state trading enterprises (STEs), although most have concentrated on theoretical aspects. Only a few[1] have used a case study approach and even these have had very limited coverage. Accordingly, while there is strong interest in the operations of STEs, especially in the context of the next round of international trade negotiations, only limited information exists on individual STEs and it is generally poorly organised. One of the main purposes of this report is to fill this information gap.

Much of the work on state trading in recent years attempts to establish a taxonomy or classification of STEs related to the degree of market distortion likely to arise from their activities.[2] As will be explained later, however, there is disagreement between studies as to what constitutes the appropriate benchmark to capture market or trade distorting effects. This report collects information on individual STEs on the basis of criteria used in a number of previous studies while avoiding those criteria that involve subjective judgements or that contain arbitrary cut-off rules. While the study does not go so far as to establish an overall taxonomy of STEs, it assembles a large amount of information about the operation of individual STEs and organises that information around a number of objective criteria that are pertinent to the issue of potential market or trade distortion.

This section is structured as follows. The definition and coverage of STEs to be used are determined in section II. Section III reviews previous studies relating to STE classification and draws some conclusions concerning the approach to be taken in the present study. Section IV provides a set of objective criteria and a taxonomy or classification within each criteria to which the individual STEs surveyed for this study are assigned. Section V presents the results of a statistical analysis that attempts to estimate market share of each

STE defined in terms of domestic sales, and of domestic and world imports or exports as appropriate, for the products in which it is involved.

Coverage of STE

Definition of STE

Article XVII of the GATT 1947 sets out that when a WTO member "establishes or maintains a state enterprise…or grants to any enterprise…exclusive or special privileges such enterprise, shall, in its purchases or sales, involving either imports or exports, act in a manner consistent with the general provisions of non-discriminatory treatment. The article, however, does not define either "state enterprise" or "privileges". The Understanding on Interpretation of Article XVII established as a result of the Uruguay Round provides the following working definition for state enterprises:

> *"…governmental and non-governmental enterprises, including marketing boards, which have been granted exclusive or special rights or privileges, including statutory or constitutional powers, in the exercise of which they influence through their purchases or sales the level or direction of imports or exports."*

The definition is still not clear, raising such questions as "What is a governmental institution or an enterprise?" "How does one define exclusive or special rights or privileges?" "Must an entity make purchases or sales itself to qualify as an STE?" Although each member must notify the WTO of any state trading enterprise within its jurisdiction, the lack of a precise definition combined with the reliance on self-notification has allowed different nations to have different views of the meaning of "state enterprise" and "exclusive and special privilege." As a result of different interpretations by member countries, views differ on precisely which organisations should be notified to the WTO. For example, it is sometimes claimed that the European Union intervention agencies[3] and the United States' marketing orders[4] for various horticultural products and for dairy products should be notified.[5]

These issues are not likely to be settled under the current WTO provisions because of the ambiguous definition, which seems to have resulted from the WTO negotiating process itself over a long period. The WTO has, in recent years, made several attempts to approach this issue resulting in a revised questionnaire and notification process, and an illustrative list of relationships between governments and state trading[6].

In the absence of a viable alternative and notwithstanding the ambiguities mentioned above, the current working definitions under the WTO provision will be applied here. Accordingly, only STEs dealing with agro-forestry products that have been notified by the OECD Member Countries in the WTO notification process are covered. STEs dealing with alcohol, manufactured tobacco and fishery products are not included.

Specific STEs covered in Part II

WTO members are required to submit new and full notifications on state trading every three years and to bring these notifications up to date in the intervening years. New, full notifications were supposed to be made in 1995 and 1998. However, the full, new notifications, based on the 1998 notification form established by the WTO, have not been fully completed. Over the period 1995-1999 a total of 41 WTO Members notified approximately 150 STEs. Of these, the STEs that deal with agro-forestry commodities in OECD Member countries are listed in Table II.1. This table shows that 11 OECD countries have notified approximately 37 STEs to the WTO.

In general, this report includes the information available from full, new notifications based on the 1998 form, received by the WTO up to the end of 1999. However, New Zealand notified changes in some of its state trading enterprises in September 2000. The Raspberry Marketing Council (RMC) has been abolished, and the Game Industry Board and the New Zealand Meat Board have ceased to be state trading enterprises. These entities are, therefore, no longer covered. However, it has not been possible to update references to the Apple and Pear Marketing Board and the Kiwifruit Marketing Board notified to the WTO, following recent legislative changes. Neither has the New Zealand Horticulture Export Authority – an entity notified as a state trading enterprise at the same time – been included in the present report.

Table II.1. List of STEs dealing with agri-forestry commodities notified to the WTO

Country	STE	Notification Year	Remarks
Australia (12)	Australian Dairy Corporation (ADC)	1995/96/97	
	Australian Dried Fruits Board (ADFB)	1995/96/97	
	Australian Honey Bureau (AHB)	1995/96/97	
	Australian Horticultural Corporation (AHC)	1995/96/97	
	Australian Meat and Livestock Corporation /Meat and Livestock Australia Ltd (AMLC / MLA)	1995/96/97	
	Australian Wheat Board (AWB)	1995/96/97	
	Wool International	1995/96/97	
	/WoolStock Australia Limited (WI / WSAL)	1995/96/97	
	Queensland Sugar Corporation (QSC)	1996/97	No longer an STE
	GRAINCO	1996/97	
	New South Wales Grains Board (NSWGB)	1996/97	
	Australian Barley Board (ABB)	1996/97	
	Grain Pool of Western Australia (GPWA)	1996/97	
	New South Wales Rice Marketing Board (RMB)		
Canada (3)	Canadian Dairy Commission (CDC)	1995/96/97	
	Canadian Wheat Board (CWB)	1995/96/97	
	Ontario Bean Producers' Marketing Board (OBPMB)	1996/97	
Czech Republic (1)	State Fund for Market Regulation (SFMR)	1995	
Japan* (3)	Japan Tobacco Inc. (JTI)	1995/96/97/98	
	Japan Food Agency (JFA)	1995/96/97/98	
	Japan Agriculture and Livestock Industries Corporation (JALIC)	1995/96/97/98	
Korea* (7)	Ministry of Agriculture and Forestry (MAF)	1995/96/97/98	
	Agricultural and Fishery Marketing Corporation (AFMC)	1995/96/97/98	
	Livestock Products Marketing Organisation (LPMO)	1995/96/97/98	
	National Livestock Cooperatives Federation (NLCF)	1995/96/97/98	
	Cheju Citrus Growers' Agricultural Cooperative (CCGAC)	1995/96/97/98	
	Korea Ginseng Cooperative Federation (KGCF)	1995/96/97/98	
	National Forestry Cooperatives Federation (NFCF)		

(Table 1 continued)

Country	STE	Notification Year	Remarks
New Zealand* (4)	Apple and Pear Marketing Board (APMB)	1995/96/97/98	
	Hop Marketing Board (HMB)	1995/96/97/98	
	New Zealand Dairy Board (NZDB)	1995/96/97/98	
	Raspberry Marketing Council (RMC)	1995/96/97/98	Abolished in 1999
	Kiwifruit Marketing Board (KMB)	1995/96/97/98	
	Game Industry Board (GIB)	1995/96/97/98	No longer an STE
	New Zealand Meat Board (NZMB)	1995/96/97/98	No longer an STE
	New Zealand Wool Board (NZWB)	1995/96/97/98	No longer an STE
Norway*	Statkorn Ltd	1995/96	No longer an STE
Poland (1)	Agricultural Marketing Agency (AMA)	1995	
Switzer-land* (1)	Swiss Butter Supply Board (BUTYRA)	1995/96/97/	No longer an STE
	Federation Office of Agriculture (FOA)	2000	
Turkey*	Turkish Soil Product Office (Turkish Grain Board)	1995/97	No longer an STE
United States (1)	Commodity Credit Corporation (CCC)	1995/96/97	

Notes:
An asterisk (*) denotes countries that made a full, new notification based on the 1998 notification form prepared by the WTO.
"No longer an STE" is indicated when a country has notified or confirmed that an organisation is no longer an STE. Because the Raspberry Marketing Council has been abolished, and the Game Industry Board, the New Zealand Wool Board and the New Zealand Meat Board are no longer STEs, they are not referred to in the rest of the document.
In some cases, a country may simply state that there has been no change from the previous notification.
Source: WTO, Notifications on State Trading Enterprises by Member Countries, various years.

Previous studies on STE classification

Study by Ingco and Ng (1998)[7]

   The analysis is based on information from various sources including WTO country notifications and Trade Policy Reviews, agriculture and commodity reports prepared by trade attaches in the Foreign Agricultural

Service of the US Department of Agriculture (USDA/FAS), and World Bank country documents and internal reports.

This paper evaluates the extent of STE control and potential distortionary effects on trade on the basis of several indicators, namely (1) the number of commodities covered under STE operations; (2) market share of STEs in key products; (3) whether the STE has monopoly control or exclusive rights; and (4) the existence of non-tariff measures used by the STEs. Based on these indicators, this paper ranks the operations of STEs in individual countries as "strong", "medium" and "weak".

- A *"strong"* status implies that the country has a long list of commodities (over 30 product categories) under extensive STE control, with exclusive rights or import or export monopoly on many items, and with significant market share in key products.

- The category *"weak"* means that only one or two sectors or a few commodities (less than five product items) are under STE control. In addition, the STE concerned may not have exclusive rights or monopoly preference on imports or such rights have been in a process of phase-out or deregulation under a government reform program.

- The category *"medium"* is in between the strong and weak category. The country still maintains STEs in trade with quite a few commodities covered and exclusive rights or monopoly power are applied to certain items (between 5 to 30 product items).

Instead of ranking and classifying individual STEs, this paper tries to rank STE operations and potential distortionary effects by country. In all, 45 developing countries are covered.

Study by the WTO Secretariat (1995)[8]

This paper is based on the information contained in notifications made under Article XVII and in GATT Trade Policy Reviews. This paper points out that the terminology used in different countries' notifications to denote various types of state trading enterprises covers a fairly broad range. This is shown in the following sampling of terms: board, control board, control authority, supply board, marketing board, marketing committee, marketing council, state fund for market regulation, state monopoly, financial monopoly, corporation, marketing corporation, industry promotion corporation, bureau, administration, government trade administration, logistics agency, market agency, canalising agency and foreign trade enterprise.

The WTO Secretariat groups these terms into the following general categories of state trading enterprises:

- Statutory marketing boards

- Export marketing boards

- Regulatory marketing boards

- Fiscal monopolies

- Canalising agencies

- Foreign trade enterprises

- Boards or corporations resulting from nationalised industries

The precise criteria actually used in grouping STEs is not explained here. There is a possibility that some STEs could be classified into two groups because the distinction between them is not clear.

Study by Dixit and Josling (1997)[9]

Dixit and Josling believe that any classification of STEs must provide insight into the economics of market distortion. They also stress the fact that there are several elements associated with the market regime under which an STE operates and its institutional structure which determine the parastatal's capacity to distort international trade. Against this background, they suggest the following criteria: (1) Trade Balance, (2) Market Control, (3) Policy Regime, (4) Product Range, and (5) Ownership and Management Structure. Based on the market control mechanism and the policy regime faced by parastatals, they classify STEs into four types:

- *Type I* is defined as a parastatal that operates under a competitive market regime without any control over either domestic or international trade.

- *Type II* is a parastatal organisation that operates without any restrictions on external trade but maintains control over the domestic market. This category could be further disaggregated as necessary, depending on whether it deals with multiple or single commodities and based on whether it is owned by the government or producers.

- *Type III* is a parastatal that operates in a competitive domestic environment but benefits from quantitative controls on external trade. Variants of type III would depend on ownership and product structures.

- *Type IV* is a parastatal that imposes quantitative restrictions on imports and maintains control over the domestic market as well. Variants would depend on product and ownership structure.

Following the colour code established in the context of the domestic support discipline in the Uruguay Round Agreement on Agriculture, Type I and Type II STEs are classified as Green, Type III are described as Amber and Type IV as Red. Green STEs are those that are least likely to distort trade and may not need scrutiny vis-à-vis current rule violations. Amber STEs are those that allow competition in the domestic market but not in external trade; the Australian Wheat Board or the New Zealand Dairy Board have been assigned to this category. Red STEs are those which maintain control over both the domestic and external markets; the Canadian Wheat Board and BULOG (Indonesia) have been assigned to this group.[10]

Study by Ackerman et al. (1997)[11]

For exporting STEs, this paper compares the big four — CWB, NZDB, AWB and QSC — using the following criteria: (1) Market Regime, (2) Policy Regime, (3) Product Regime, and (4) Ownership Regime. For importing STEs, major STE importers from Korea (MAF, LPMO), Japan (JFA), Indonesia (BULOG) and Mexico (CONASUPO) are compared using the same set of criteria. The criteria and conclusions drawn are similar to those used in Dixit and Josling.

Study by Veeman, Fulton and Larue (1998)[12]

This study proposes that the categorisation of STEs be based on indicators of contestability, which is considered as the crucial indication of potential market power. Other relevant but subsidiary criteria are the relationship between the STE and government/politicians and whether the STE operates with an appropriate level of transparency.

The contestability indicator[13] is made up of the following elements: (1) Concentration, (2) Import Access and (3) Price Comparison. On the basis of these criteria, STEs are classified into three types.[14]

- *Type I:* The market can be regarded as contestable. This class of STE:

  - faces competition in the domestic market and controls less than 33% of domestic market sales (importing STE),

  - faces competition in the export market and controls less than 33% of export market sales (exporting STE),

  - does not have single desk status in the domestic market (exporting STE) and

  - has a single desk role in the domestic market, but the border is fully open to imports (exporting STE).

- *Type II*: This class of STE operates within market and institutional situations in which contestability may be compromised. They

  - face competition in the domestic market but control 33% or more of domestic sales (importing STE),

  - face competition in the export market but control 33% to 49% of world export sales (exporting STE) and

  - face competition in export markets and have a single desk role in the domestic market, but the border is not open to imports (exporting STE).

- *Type III: Contestability is contravened by this group of STEs:*

  - there is no competition in importation (importing STE),

  - tariff rate quota and/or minimum access commitments are administered by the STE (importing STE) and

  - they control 50% or more of world exports sales of the commodity (exporting STE).

As in the case studies by Dixit and Josling, this study also used a colour code to characterise each type of STE: Green STEs for Type I, Amber STEs for Type II and Red STEs for Type III. Under this study, the New Zealand Dairy Board, the Australian Wheat Board and the Canadian Wheat Board are classified as Green STEs of Type I, while BULOG of Indonesia, the Japanese Food Agency and Korean State Mandated Imports are categorised as Red STEs of Type III.

Implications from previous studies

The studies by Ingco and Ng and by the WTO Secretariat are not particularly useful in the context of this paper in that the former is carried out at a country level rather than at the level of the individual STE while the latter is based on an unclear distinction between the different types. The study by Ackerman *et al.* uses the same analytical framework as that by Dixit and Josling. The two major studies retained for reference are Dixit and Josling and Veeman *et al.*

As shown above, the studies by Dixit and Josling and Veeman *et al.* propose different criteria to categorise STEs, leading to different conclusions. The Veeman study appears to be rooted in the idea that the major concern on exporting STEs is not that they might hold and exert market power, but that they may be used as a means to circumvent the export subsidy discipline of the URAA. In addition to this concern is an alleged lack of transparency. In criticising the criteria proposed by Dixit and Josling, this study gives strong emphasis to "import access" criteria.

The fact that two different studies can come to such different conclusions concerning the potential of a given STE to distort trade indicates the very real difficulty in developing a set of objective criteria not subject to value judgements or to somewhat arbitrary cut-off points. This study therefore proposes a number of criteria around which the information concerning STEs can be organised. The criteria retained are a combination of those used by Dixit and Josling and those used by Veeman *et al.* In addition to eliminating criteria that involved a degree of subjectivity or arbitrariness, it was decided to retain only criterion that were potentially relevant to all or most of the STEs to be considered and for which the relevant data could be found or estimated. With respect to certain individual criteria, a categorisation is proposed (for example under the criterion of trade balance, an STE is defined as an importer, exporter or both), with respect to others the summary data are reported (for example, share of domestic market). No attempt is made at this stage to develop an overall ranking or taxonomy permitting individual STEs to be assigned according to degrees of potential or actual market or trade distortion. This reflects the more modest purpose of this study, which is to assemble an inventory containing the maximum amount of comparable information about the operation of STEs in OECD countries.

Criteria for inventory and taxonomy

Criteria set and rationale

As explained above, elements are adopted from the format provided by Dixit and Josling and Veeman *et al.* Information is assembled around the following four headings. Trade Balance and Market Control; Policy Regime; Product Range and Appropriate Transparency; and Ownership and Relationship with Government.

Criteria 1: Trade balance and market control

Trade balance

Trade balance refers to whether an STE is an exporter or an importer. Because the definition of a state enterprise is unclear, the definition of an exporting or importing STE is also unclear. We have nonetheless decided to adopt the existing definition from the WTO implying that an exporting or importing STE is one that has been granted exclusive or special rights or privileges relating to exports or imports respectively. The behaviour of exporting STEs can be expected to be very different from importing STEs. Whereas an STE exporter attempts to enhance trade and competition in the international market, an STE importer is interested in restricting trade and augmenting protection in the domestic market (Dixit and Josling, 1997).

Market control

Market control relates to specific activities that a STE might be engaged in. Dixit and Josling (1997) proposed four specific activities, such as imports, exports, domestic procurement (purchase), and domestic marketing (sales), in the belief that the ability of an STE to distort international trade depends on the control it exercises over these activities. On the contrary, Veeman (1998) did not regard this as a useful criterion because it sheds light only on the potential scope of STE operations, rather than providing evidence on the actual degree of market control exercised by an individual STE.

Clearly, involvement in exports and domestic procurement (purchase) is more relevant for an exporting STE, and imports and domestic marketing (sales) in the case of an importing STE. Thus, by combining trade balance criteria with market control criteria, this paper investigates *control of imports* and *control of domestic marketing* in the case of importing STEs and *control of exports* and **control of domestic procurement** in the case of exporting STEs. Some agricultural exporting countries have maintained state trading enterprises, which have the exclusive right to export domestic products, the exclusive right to sell in the domestic market and which also play a role with respect to imports. In this case, all four activities relative to market control are investigated.[15]

Criteria 2: Policy regime

This encompasses three elements — trade policy instruments, domestic policy instruments under control of individual STEs, and policy measures that grant a competitive edge to an STE. The scope of each of these elements is potentially very wide and there is a danger of arbitrary selection of instruments. The possibility of differing views on the importance of these criteria exists, as shown in Dixit and Josling and in Veeman *et al.*[16] With respect to policy regime, as with the other criteria, this paper reports only objective non-controversial information available for all or most of the STEs being studied.

The discussion under each of the headings which follow should be interpreted carefully. In particular it is important to distinguish between the effects of the state trading enterprise itself and the effects of the trade or domestic policy instruments which it operates or administers on behalf of the government. In many cases these instruments would be in place anyway, irrespective of the existence or otherwise of the state trading enterprise. This point is a key one in exploring the possible impact of state trading and is explored fully in Part I.

Trade policy instruments

With respect to **trade policy instruments**, two different approaches are applied depending on the status of each STE in terms of trade balance. For exporting STEs, export subsidies and officially supported export credits[17] are obviously more important than protective border measures. On the other hand, as importing STEs are more interested in restricting trade and augmenting protection in the domestic market, border protection measures are deemed to be major trade policy instruments. Border protection measures to be reviewed are quantitative restrictions and/or tariffs on imports of commodities under the control of specific STEs. For the purposes of this paper, the tariff rate quotas[18] introduced in the tariffication process of the URAA are considered as quantitative restrictions. This is because the very high tariff rates applying to over tariff rate quota quantities are often prohibitive, with the result that the TRQs have the same effect as an import quota.

Domestic policy instruments

In regard to **domestic policy instruments**, there is a wide choice of instruments. For example, Dixit and Josling compared income payments with market price support. This report relies on whether products are notified as having "Product-Specific AMS"[19] (Aggregate Measurement of Support) in the context of the discipline on domestic support of the URAA. This information is easily available from the WTO schedules and notifications. In addition, there is the question as to whether the Product-Specific AMS identified arises from a market price support policy or not.

Competitive edge

STEs may gain a **competitive edge** because of exclusive access to certain policy instruments that favour STEs compared to other firms operating in the same market. However, in practice, defining and identifying such measures is difficult

Criteria 3: Product range and transparency

Product range

Product range denotes the scope of products and activities in which individual STEs are involved. Views differ concerning whether product range might be a reasonable indicator of the capacity of a firm to distort trade. Dixit and Josling regard it as potentially important in the belief that market power depends on a firm's capacity to differentiate its product and regulate use of substitutes, whereas Veeman *et al.* do not find this criteria to be of any great significance. It is nonetheless included in this paper as it is non-controversial in itself and simply provides general information related to the operations of individual STEs. Two aspects are included: one is the range of products, the other is involvement in upstream and downstream activities.

Transparency

Although transparency is a potentially useful criterion against which to judge the potential of an STE to distort trade, it is difficult in practice to define an objective indicator. As suggested in Veeman *et al.* we limit ourselves to asking whether information is regularly made available to the public on the operation of the STE, which is equivalent in scope and detail to the information available from major competitors of the STE.

Criteria 4: Ownership and relationship with government

Even though it is debatable whether ownership and relationship with government is an appropriate indicator of the potential of an STE to distort trade, this indicator does provide useful information on the legal and institutional status of individual STEs. Under this criteria, facts concerning ownership and financial status of STEs are recorded.

Information listed under criteria

This section presents a summary of the information assembled under the different criteria. The information sought or variable estimated under each criteria is summarised in Table II.2, which also gives an indication of the source of the information under the various headings. Tables II.3 to II.12 contain the summary information itself. The acronyms introduced in Table II.1 for individual STEs are used throughout these tables. Section V contains the results of an exercise designed to estimate the domestic and world market shares of individual STEs in the commodities they handle.

Data source

Notifications on STEs to the WTO are the main source of data[20]. Notifications to the WTO on domestic support and export subsidies have also been drawn upon. Previous studies on TRQs, *WTO Trade Policy Reviews* and *OECD Monitoring and Evaluation Reports* are referred to. Web-sites of individual STEs were explored as a supplementary source of information. In all cases, the most recently available data are used.

Table II.2. Information collected under each criteria and source

Criteria		Investigated questions	Major source
Trade balance and market control	**Control of imports**	• What is the status of the STE concerning imports: single desk authority to import? Or actual importer (or manager) of TRQ? Or having only the right to issue importing licenses? • What market share of national imports (or world imports) is controlled by the STE?	• Notifications on STEs to WTO • Estimation in Section V • Web-site • Study on specific country
	Control of domestic marketing	• What is the status of the STE as to domestic marketing: Does the STE have monopoly power over domestic marketing of imported products and domestic products? Or only monopoly in respect of one aspect? Or no monopoly power at all? • What share of domestic market sales for each of the products it deals with is controlled by the STE?	• Notifications on STEs to WTO • Estimation in Section V • OECD Monitoring Report
	Control of exports	• What is the status of the STE regarding exports: sole export seller? Or having only the right to issue export licenses? • What share of exports is controlled by the STE? • What is the share of world export sales that is controlled by the STE?	• Notifications on STEs to WTO • Estimation in Section V • Web-site • Study on specific country

Table II.2. Information collected under each criteria and source *(cont.)*

Trade balance and market control	**Control of domestic procurement**	• What is the status of the STE as to domestic procurement: Does the STE have monopsony power in purchasing for export as well as for domestic sale? Or only monopsony in one of export or domestic sales? Or no monopsony power at all? • What share of domestic procurement for each of the products it deals with is controlled by the STE?	• Notifications on STEs to WTO • Estimation in Section V • OECD monitoring report
Policy regime	**Trade policy instruments**	• Whether border protection relies on quantitative restrictions (including tariff rate quota) on imports or on tariffs? • Are export subsidies granted to products under control of the STE? • Are officially supported export credits granted to products under control of the STE?[1]	• Notifications on export subsidy to WTO • OECD Study on TRQ (1999*b* and *c*), OECD monitoring • WTO trade policy reviews • Confidential survey conducted by the Participants to the Arrangement on Guidelines for Officially Supported Export Credits
	Domestic policy instruments	• Whether "Product-Specific AMS" in a WTO context is given to products under control of the STE? • If given, is it market price support or some other policy? • Are there other relevant domestic policies administered by the STE?	• Notifications on domestic support to WTO • OECD monitoring report
	Competitive edge	• Are there preferential arrangements such as loan guarantees or debt forgiveness that are equivalent to subsidies?	• Notifications on STEs to WTO • Web-site

Table II.2. Information collected under each criteria and source (*cont.*)

Product range and transparency	Product range	• Which commodities does the STE handle and/or control? • Does the STE engage in and/or control upstream and downstream activities[2]?	Notifications on STE to WTO Web-site
	Appropriate transparency	• Is information regularly made available to the public on the operations of the STE?	Notifications on STEs to WTO
Ownership and relationship with government		• Is the STE is owned by the government or by producers? • Are the operations of the STE independent of government? • Is the STE self-financing?	Notifications on STEs to WTO Web-site and others

Notes:
1. See note 17.
2. With respect to this item, it is important to note two different cases: one is the case that STE is conducting downstream and/or upstream activities, the other is the case that STE is influencing those sectors without directly carrying out those activities.

Taxonomy of STE by criteria

As explained above, this paper stops short of proposing an overall taxonomy or ranking based on the actual or potential trade distorting effect of individual STEs. However, within the various criteria a taxonomy is sometimes proposed.

Taxonomy based on criteria 1: Trade balance and market control. STEs are first classified into exporting or importing STEs. This classification reflects only whether the STE has been granted exclusive or special rights relating to exports or imports and does not necessarily mean that the STE itself directly imports or exports. Exporting STEs are then investigated with respect to control of exports and control of domestic procurement while importing STEs are looked into with respect to control of imports and control of domestic marketing. Of a total of 36 STEs covered, 23 are classified as exporting STEs, 11 are classified as importing STEs. This information is summarised in Table II.3.

Table II.3. Exporting STEs and Importing STEs

Exporting STEs	Importing STEs
Australia (12): ABB, ADC, ADFB, AHB, AHC, AMLC/MLA, QSC, AWB, GPWA, NSWGB, RMB, WI/WSAL	Canada (1): CDC
	Japan (3): JALIC, JFA, JTI
Canada (3): CWB, OBPMB	Korea (7): AFMC, CCGAC, KGCF, LPMO, MAF, NLCF, NFCF
New Zealand (7): APMB, NZDB, HMB, KMB	
Czech Republic (1): SFMR	Switzerland (1): FOA
Poland (1): AMA	
United States (1): CCC*	

*   The CCC does not have any special or exclusive rights with respect to exports and has not actually engaged in exports since 1995, but it retains authority to export.

Table II.4 explains the further classification of exporting STEs with respect to degree of control over exports and domestic procurement and identifies three different cases. The number 1 generally denotes the strongest degree of control.

Table II.4. Characteristics of exporting STE with respect to export control and domestic procurement

Type	Export control aspect (ECA)	Type	Domestic procurement control aspect (DPC)
1	Sole exporter	1	Monopsony buyer in purchasing for export as well as for domestic marketing
2	Engaged in actual export activities which may include granting export subsidies and/or issuing export licenses	2	Monopsony buyer in purchasing for export with or without a share in domestic marketing
3	Having only the right to issue export licenses	3	All cases other than type 1 and type 2

The taxonomy or classification as it applies to STEs covered is shown in Table II.5. Theoretically, there are nine possible combinations of the different export control and domestic procurement aspects but, in fact, only five actually occur. It is important to note that the status of individual STEs may differ by commodity. For each STE, the share in national exports, world exports and domestic procurement is estimated and shown in Section V.

79

Table II.5. Typology of exporting STEs with respect to export control and domestic procurement

ECA Type	DPC Type	STE	Ratio
1	1	RMB (rice) HMB (hops)	2/24
1	2	ABB[4] (barley, oats) QSC (sugar) AWB (wheat) GPWA[3] (barley, oilseeds) NSWGB[3] (barley, oats, oilseeds, sorghum) OBPMB[4] (beans) APMB (apples, pears) NZDB (butter, cheese, anhydrous milkfat, skimmed milk powder, whole milk powder, casein) KMB (kiwifruit)	9/24
2	2	CWB (barley), wheat,	1/24
2	3	ADC[1] (cheese) WI/WSAL (wool) SFMR[2] (butter, cheese, skim milk powder) AMA (wheat, rye, butter, skim milk powder) CCC[4] (coarse grain, butter, skim milk powder, cheese), CDC (butter, skimmed milk powder, whole milk powder, evaporated milk)	7/24
3	3	ADC[1] (butter, anhydrous milk, skim milk powder, whole milk powder) ADFB (dried vine fruit) AHB (honey) AHC (apples, avocado, citrus, pears) AMLC/MLA (beef, sheepmeat and goat, lamb) SFMR[2] (wheat)	6/24

Notes: 1. & 2. The status of ADC and SFMR differs by commodity.
3. Since each of these is sole seller in a limited geographical area, the share in national exports is not 100%.
4. The CCC provides finance to private exporters but does not itself "grant" the export subsidies. This is done by FAS/USDA.

Table II.6 explains the further classification of importing STEs with respect to degree of control over imports and domestic marketing, also identifying three different cases with respect to each element. Once again, the number 1 generally denotes the strongest degree of control.

Table II.6. Characteristics of importing STEs with respect to import control and domestic marketing

Type	Import control aspect (ICA)	Type	Domestic marketing control aspect (DMC)
1	Single desk importer[1]	1	Monopoly supplier in domestic sale of domestic products
2	Only importer (or manager) of tariff rate quota[2]	2	Holder of some share in domestic sale of domestic products
3	Right to issue import licenses only	3	No involvement in domestic sale of domestic products

Notes:
1. This category is limited to sole importers of commodities subject to import restrictions. As a consequence of tariffication in the UR, this is rare.
2. Although over-quota tariffs are so high in many cases that it is not easy to import over-quota, this is different from the sole importer case in that other entities can in principle import.

Table II.7 shows the typology of importing STEs based on the categories presented in Table II.6. Considering the two aspects of import control and domestic marketing control, out of a possible nine combinations five actually occur. As in the case of exporting STEs, individual STEs may change status according to the commodity in question. For each STE, the respective share in national imports, world imports and domestic sales is estimated below.

Table II.7. Typology of importing STEs with respect to import control and domestic marketing

ICA Type	DMC Type	STE	Ratio
1	2	MAF[1] (rice)	1/15
1	3	JTI (leaf tobacco)	1/15
2	2	JALIC[2] (raw silk) JFA (barley, rice, wheat) AFMC[3] (buckwheat, garlic, groundnuts, onions, soybean) CCGAC (orange) NFCF (pine nuts), CDC (butter)	6/15
2	3	JALIC[2] (skim milk powder, whey) AFMC[3] (ginger, potatoes, sesame seed) KGCF (ginseng) LPMO (beef) MAF[1] (barley) NLCF (honey)	6/15
3	3	FOA (bread flour, durum wheat meal)	1/15

Notes: 1. 2. & 3.   The status of MAF, JALIC and AFMC differ by commodity.

Taxonomy based on criteria 2: policy regime. First, the distinction between exporting and importing STEs is retained. A taxonomy is then proposed. For exporting STEs, it is based on involvement in the administration of export subsidies, officially supported export credits, and policies leading to Product-Specific AMS. For importing STEs, it is based on quantitative import restrictions and domestic support. Table II.8 shows the results for exporting STEs and also reveals that individual STE differ in status by commodity.

**Table II.8. Characteristics of exporting STEs with respect
to export subsidies and domestic support**

Export subsidy	Domestic support	STE	Ratio
Yes[4]	Yes	SFMR[1]* (milk and dairy products) CCC[3] (dairy products*, coarse grains)	2/26
Yes	No[4]	AMA[2] (sugar, potato starch) CCC[3] (poultrymeat)	2/26
No	Yes	ADC (milk) AWB (wheat) CDC* (milk including butter and skim milk powder) CWB (wheat, barley) OBPMB (dry bean) SFMR[1]* (wheat) AMA[2]* (wheat, rye, honey) CCC[3] (peanuts*, sugar*)	8/26
No	No	ADFB (dried vine fruit) AHB (honey) AHC (all products including apples and pears) MLA (meat, livestock) WSAL (wool) QSC (raw sugar) NSWGB (barley, oats, oilseed, sorghum) ABB (barley) GPWA (barley, lupins, canola) RMB (rice) APMB (apples, pears) HMB (hops) NZDB (dairy products) KMB (kiwifruit)	14/26

Notes: 1. 2. & 3. Classification changes by commodity.

4. "Yes" denotes that export subsidies and/or domestic support are granted, while "No" denotes the opposite. In the case of the CCC, it does not itself grant export subsidies. This is done by FAS/USDA, while CCC provides the finance.
5. An asterisk (*) denotes an STE and/or commodity for which domestic support takes the form of market price support.

Officially supported export credits are another possible policy tool for exporting STEs. The participants to the Arrangement on Guidelines for Officially Supported Export Credits conducted a confidential survey, and granted permission for limited use of the data for the present study. According to the survey, only the CCC is directly involved in officially supported export credits for agricultural products. It supplies financing in respect of export credit programmes run by FAS/USDA. According to the survey, officially supported export credits are available in other countries with exporting STEs, including

Australia, Canada, Czech Republic, and Poland, but the STEs in those countries do not administer them. Nonetheless, STEs in some countries may be involved in export credit activity.

Table II.9 presents a taxonomy for importing STEs based on quantitative restrictions and domestic support. With respect to Tables II.8 and II.9, attention should be paid to the fact that an individual STE may change status with respect to domestic support or export subsidies from year to year.

Table II.9. Characteristics of importing STEs with respect to quantitative import restrictions and domestic support

QR[3]	Domestic support	STE	Ratio
Yes[4]	Yes	CDC* (butter) JFA* (rice, wheat, barley) JALIC* (dairy products, raw silk) MAF (rice, barley) AFMC[1](soybean*, garlic, potato) LPMO* (beef) CCGAC (orange, Korean citrus*) KGCF (ginseng roots)	8/13
Yes	No[4]	AFMC[1] (all other products except soybean, garlic and potato) NLCF (natural honey) NFCF (pine nuts)	3/13
No	Yes	Nothing	0/13
No	No	JTI (leaf tobacco) FOA[2] (bread flour)	2/13

Notes:
1. Classification changes by commodity.
2. For wheat, Switzerland maintains a tariff rate quota as well as market price support.
3. As explained earlier, this includes tariff rate quota (TRQ).
4. "Yes" denotes that domestic support and/or quantitative restriction exist, while "No" denotes the opposite.
5. An asterisk (*) denotes an STE and/or commodity for which domestic support takes the form of market price support.

Taxonomy based on criteria 3. Product Range and Transparency. Under this criteria, the classification is made without a prior distinction being made between exporting and importing STEs. Table II.10 shows whether individual STEs deal with only one product or with more than one.

Table II.10. Characteristics of STEs with respect to product coverage

Type	STE	Ratio
Single product	ADFB AHB AWB WI/WSAL QSC RMB OBPMB JTI LPMO NLCF CCGAC KGCF NFCF HMB KMB FOA	16/33
Multiple product	ADC AHC AMLC/MLA NSWGB ABB GPWA CDC CWB SFMR JFA JALIC MAF AFMC APMB NZDB AMA CCC	17/33

Note   For the present purposes, "upstream" and "downstream" are defined, in terms of the production process, as activities that are closer to ("upstream") or further from ("downstream") basic extraction or manufacture than the product in question.

Table II.1 reveals the level of individual STEs' involvement in downstream and/or upstream activities. Three possible case are identified. In the first case, the STE influences upstream and downstream activities but does not actually engage in them itself. In the second case, the STE influences upstram and downstream activities but does not actually engage in them itself. Lastly, the STE neither carries out nor influences upstream or downstream activities.

Table II.11. Characteristics of STEs with respect to upstream and downstream activities

Type	STE	Ratio
Control over and/or engages in upstream or downstream activities	ADC AWB JTI AFMC KGCF APMB NZDB CCC	8/33
Influence on upstream or downstream activities	ADFB QSC RMB CDC CWB OBPMB SFMR JALIC HMB AMA	10/33
No relationship with upstream or downstream activities	AHB AHC AMLC/MLA WI/WSAL NSWGB ABB GPWA JFA MAF LPMO NLCF CCGAC NFCF KMB FOA	15/33

Taxonomy based on criteria 4. Ownership and relationship with Government. Under this criteria, the classification is made on the basis of the relationship between the STE and government as shown in Table II.12 without distinction between exporting and importing STEs. Based on the detailed information contained in the inventory, three types of relationship to government are once again identified (those used in WTO, 1998). In the first case, the STE is a branch of government; that is, it is itself a government institution. In the second case, the STE is owned fully or partially by government. If an STE falls into both categories it is assigned to the first[21]. In the last case, the STE is entirely separate from government.

Table II.12. Characteristics of STEs with respect to relationship with government

Type	STE	Ratio
A branch of government	SFMR RMB JFA MAF AMA FOA CCC	7/33
Owned, fully or partially, by government	ADC ADFB AHB AHC QSC NSWGB GPWA CDC JALIC AFMC	10/33
Separate from government[1]	AMLC/MLA AWB WI/WSAL ABB CWB OBPMB JTI LPMO NLCF CCGAC KGCF NFCF APMB HMB NZDB KMB	16/33

Estimation of market share by STE

Introduction

McCorriston and MacLaren (Part I) draw attention to the importance of the benchmark against which the potential trade distorting effects of STEs should be assessed. In particular, they suggest that a perfectly competitive benchmark in which only state trading enterprises distort competition is unlikely to be correct. In this section, an attempt is made to estimate the degree of market power exercised by STEs in domestic and world markets by developing some simple indicators of market share. Clearly, it would be essential to gather information on other big players, particularly private firms, in order to gauge the extent of competition in the markets concerned. In any event, market share should not be interpreted as an unambiguous indication of the exercise of market power. Information on the market share of the STE itself is only a first step in this process.

Data set and basic methodology

Two basic data sets are used: country notifications on state trading enterprises to the WTO and the FAO data base on production, consumption and trade in agricultural commodities. A two-tier approach is applied. First, some empirical information is collected on each STE from country notifications to the WTO, supplemented and sometimes updated with information from the STEs web-sites. Information on the share of each STE in national exports (CEe), domestic procurement (MSp), national imports (CEm) and domestic marketing of domestically produced products ($CEdm$) is assembled in this way. In principle, values obtained are the average of the most recent three years available.

This information is then combined with the data from the FAO data base (average values for the period 1995-97) to give: share of STE in world exports ($CEwe$), share of STE in world imports ($CEwm$) and market share of STE in domestic marketing (MSm). For some STEs it was possible to derive the information for MSp and MSm directly from data provided in the country notifications, while in others it was not. For all STEs, MSp or MSm was calculated using a standard formula, but where possible, the figure arrived at from the notification is also included in the relevant tables. Differences between the two figures would be due to differences in the data used. Some of the limitations of the data are outlined below, and in general, where the information concerning MSp and MSm is derived from the notifications, it is likely to be more accurate.

Exporting STEs

For exporting STEs, the share of each STE in national exports, world exports and domestic procurement is calculated or estimated by the following procedures. The results are shown in Table II.13.

Share of STE in national exports (CEe): The value of CEe depends on the status of the individual STE.

Table II.13. Value of CEe

Type	Case	Value of *Cee*
1	STE is sole exporter	$CEe=1$
2	STE is engaging in actual exporting activities which may include export subsidies and/or issuing export licenses. *CEe* is determined empirically from data such as country notifications.	$0<CEe<1$
3	STE has the right only to issue export licenses.	$CEe=0$

Share of STE in world exports (CEwe): This is calculated from the following equation:

$$CEwe = (Ce / We)*CEe,$$

Where, Ce is specific country exports and We is world exports for the specific commodity.

Share of STE in domestic procurement (MSp)

The value of *MSp* is determined by the STE's status with respect to domestic procurement. In the case of Type 2 and Type 3, *MSp* is determined either directly from the data (e.g. country notifications to the WTO) or by the following equation:

$$MSp= \{(Ce / Pd)*CEe\} + Sdm,$$

Where, Pd is domestic production, Ce is national exports, Sdm is STE's share in domestic procurement for domestic sale (marketing).

Although theoretically an STE could have monopsony power over domestic marketing only, this possibility is ruled out because it is irrelevant to the exporting STE case.

Table II.14. Value of MSp

Type	Case	Value of MSp
1	An STE has monopsony power in purchasing for export as well as for domestic marketing (sale).	$MSp=1$
2	While the STE has monopsony power in purchasing for export, it has only some or no share in procurement for domestic marketing.	$0 \leq MSp<1$
3	All other cases	

Importing STEs

For importing STE's, the share of each STE in national imports, world imports and domestic marketing (sales) is calculated or estimated by the following procedures, the results of which are shown in Table II.15.

Share of STE in imports (CEm) The value of *CEm* depends on the status of the individual STE as follows. For Type 2, an estimate might be available from the STE itself (notification or other source). If not, *CEm* is calculated by the following equation using the OECD trade database:

$CEm = TRQm / Cm,$

Where, TRQm is actual TRQ imports and Cm is total imports.

Table II.15. Value of CEm

Type	Case	Value of *Cem*
1	The STE has sole authority to import.	$CEm=1$
2	The STE controls imports under the tariff rate quotas (TRQs).	$0<CEm\leq 1$
3	The STE only issues importing licenses.	$CEm=0$

Share of STE in world imports (CEwm): This is calculated from the following equation:

$$CEwm = (Cm / Wm)*CEm,$$

Where, Cm is total country imports and Wm is world imports for a given commodity.

Share of STE in domestic marketing (MSm) *MSm* can be found either directly from country notifications to the WTO, or can be calculated from the equation below:

$$MSm = \{(Cm*CEm) / Cd\} + [\{(Pd-Ce)*CEdm\} / Cd],$$

Where, Cd is domestic consumption, Cm is total imports, CEm is share of STE in total imports, Pd is domestic production, Ce is total exports and CEdm is share of STE in domestic marketing of domestically produced products.

With respect to the value of *CEdm*, there are three possibilities. In Case 2, the actual value of *CEdm* is determined by reference to the data. However, the share of the STEs purchases in domestic production can be used as a proxy if the data are not available.

Table II.16. Value of CEdm

Type	Case	Value of *Cedm*
1	The STE is a monopoly supplier of domestically produced products.	$CEdm=1$
2	The STE holds some share in domestic marketing of domestically produced products.	$0<CEdm<1$
3	STE does not engage in domestic sale of domestically produced products.	$CEdm=0$

Limitations

The estimates in this section should be interpreted carefully because of differences in the source and definitions of the data used. For example, the FAO data base on trade, production and consumption is based on the third revision of the United Nations Standard International Trade Classification (SITC Rev.3), which groups commodities according to the degree of processing they have undergone. In contrast, the WTO notification data are usually on the basis of the Harmonized System, a World Customs Organisation system which groups goods according to their component materials, from raw materials through to processed and manufactured products. These differences could lead to some over or underestimation. Also, the period used in the individual data source can differ. Some data are based on calendar years, some on fiscal years, while others are based on a marketing year. This too could lead to some inaccuracy in the estimates.

Table II.17. Importing STE: Average 1995-97

STE	Country	Product	National imports (MT)	World imports (MT)	Domestic consumption (MT)	Share of STE in national imports (%)	Share of national imports in world imports (%)	Share of STE in world imports (%)	Share of national imports in consumption (%)	Share of STE in domestic sales of domestic products	Share of STE in domestic sale (%)	Notification
			C_m	W_m	C_d	CE_m $= 0$ $= 100$ $0 < CE_m \le 100$	C_m/W_m	CE_m^* (C_m/W_m)	C_m/C_d	MS_m $=100$ $=0$ $0<CE_{dm}<100$	$=[CE_m^*(C_m/C_d)+C_{edm}^*(P_d-C_e)/C_d)]$	
CDC	Canada	Butter, Ghee	2 250	1 281 221	85 255	100.0 (2)	0.2	0.2	2.6	100.0 (2)	n.a.	100
JALIC	Japan	Milk, skimmed	1 018 350	25 515 217	3 017 317	87 (2)	4.0	3.5	33.8	0.0 (3)	0.0	-
JALIC	Japan	Whey,modified whey	n.a.	n.a.	n.a.	34.0 (2)	n.a.	n.a.	n.a.	0.0 (3)	n.a.	-
JALIC	Japan	Raw silk	4 886	39 183	10 150	6.0 (2)	12.5	0.7	48.1	10.0 (2)	8.1	6.0
JFA	Japan	Barley	2 601 094	26 458 707	2 730 473	99.0 (2)	9.8	9.7	95.3	39.0 (2)	97.4	61.0
JFA	Japan	Rice (milled equivalent)	315 453	20 219 793	8 861 568	99.0 (2)	1.6	1.5	3.6	12.0 (2)	15.2	8.0
JFA	Japan	Wheat	6 221 315	120 991 933	6 731 465	99.0 (2)	5.1	5.1	92.4	90.0 (2)	92.7	94.0
JTI	Japan	Leaf tobacco	164 355	2 683 755	217 762	100.0 (1)	6.1	6.1	75.5	0.0 (3)	75.5	-
AFMC	Korea	buckwheat	1 592	196 366	7 179	5.0 (2)	0.8	0.0	22.2	9.0 (2)	1.1	18.0
AFMC	Korea	Garlic	8 927	602 675	444 855	86.0 (2)	1.5	1.3	2.0	1.0 (2)	2.7	14.0
AFMC	Korea	Ginger	2 761	171 492	9 919	33.0 (2)	1.6	0.5	27.8	0.0 (3)	9.2	2.0
AFMC	Korea	Groundnuts (shelled equivalent)	17 819	1 523 996	25 623	31.0 (2)	1.2	0.4	69.5	7.0 (2)	23.7	14.0
AFMC	Korea	Onions	22 280	2 975 711	780 554	71.0 (2)	0.7	0.5	2.9	2.0 (2)	4.0	3.0
AFMC	Korea	Potatoes	294 669	15 439 437	947 252	100.0 (2)	1.9	1.9	31.1	0.0 (3)	31.1	1.0
AFMC	Korea	Sesame seed	58 350	580 060	89 885	98.0 (2)	10.1	9.9	64.9	0.0 (3)	63.6	65.0

Table II.17. Importing STE: Average 1995-97 (cont.)

STE	Country	Product	National imports (MT) Cm	World imports (MT) Wm	Domestic consumption (MT) Cd	Share of STE in national imports (%) CEm = 0 = 100 = 0 < CEm ≤ 100	Share of national imports in world imports (%) Cm/Wm	Share of STE in world imports (%) CEm* (Cm/Wm)	Share of national imports in consumption (%) Cm/Cd	Share of STE in domestic sales of domestic products =100 =0 =0<CEdm<100	Share of STE in domestic sale (%) MSm =[Cem*(Cm/Cd)+Cedm*(Ce/Cd)]	Notification
AFMC	Korea	Soya beans	1 501 971	34 601 587	1 551 794	80.0 (2)	4.3	3.5	96.8	2.0 (2)	77.6	55.0
CCGAC	Korea	Oranges, mandarines	526 872	19 171 067	1 093 014	100.0 (2)	2.7	2.7	48.2	- (2)	-	3.0
CCGAC	Korea	Citrus, other	50	253 367	7 037		0.0	0.0	0.7	0.0 (3)	0.0	0.0
KGCF	Korea	Ginseng	n.a.	n.a.	n.a.	45.0 (2)	n.a.	n.a.	n.a.	0.0 (3)	n.a.	1.0
LPMO	Korea	Bovine meat	206 096	6 648 256	4 070 225	61.0 (2)	3.1	1.9	5.1	0.0 (3)	3.1	26.0
MAF	Korea	Barley	178 273	26 458 707	579 696	100.0 (2)	0.7	0.7	30.8	0.0 (3)	30.8	63.0
MAF	Korea	Rice (milled equivalent)	40 711	20 219 793	4 627 390	100.0 (1)	0.2	0.2	0.9	25.0 (2)	25.9	20.0
NLCF	Korea	Honey	270	319 451	12 769	100.0 (2)	0.1	0.1	2.1	0.0 (3)	2.1	1.0
NFCF	Korea	Pine nuts	n.a.	n.a.	n.a.	100.0 (2)	n.a.	n.a.	n.a.	- (2)	-	-
FOA	Switzerland	Bread flour	476	n.a.	n.a.	- (3)	n.a.	n.a.	n.a.	- (3)	-	-
FOA	Switzerland	Durum, wheat meal	47	n.a.	n.a.	- (3)	n.a.	n.a.	n.a.	- (3)	-	-

Table II.18. Exporting STE: Average 1995-97

STE	Country	Product	National exports (MT) Ce	World exports (MT) We	Domestic production Pd	Share of STE in national exports (%) CEe =100 =0 =0<Cee<100	CEe case	Share of national exports in world exports (%) Ce/We	Share of STE in world exports (%) CEe* (Ce/We)	Share of national exports in domestic production (%) Ce/Pd	Notification	MSp case	Share of STE in domestic procurement (%) MSp =100 =Cee*(Ce/Pd)+Sdm	Notification
ABB	Australia	Barley	3 572 653	27 058 903	6 333 597	38.0	(1)	13.2	5.0	56.4	-	(2)	21.4	38.0
ABB	Australia	Oats	200 817	2 810 735	1 703 667	9.0	(1)	7.1	0.6	11.8	-	(2)	1.1	9.0
ADC	Australia	Butter, Ghee	93 960	1 328 538	142 133	0.0	(3)	7.1	0.0	66.1	44.0	(3)	0.0	0.0
ADC	Australia	Cheese	133 810	2 752 910	261 133	38.0	(2)	4.9	1.8	51.2	44.0	(3)	19.5	17.0
ADC	Australia	Anhydous milk	n.a.	n.a.	n.a.	0.0	(3)	n.a.	n.a.	n.a.	93.0	(3)	0.0	0.0
ADC	Australia	Milk, skimmed	2 214 212	22 119 330	3 016 071	0.0	(3)	10.0	0.0	73.4	75.0	(3)	0.0	0.0
ADC	Australia	Milk, whole	1 046 402	20 420 643	8 916 667	0.0	(3)	5.1	0.0	11.7	73.0	(3)	0.0	0.0
ADFB	Australia	Dried vine fruit	n.a.	n.a.	n.a.	0.0	(3)	n.a.	n.a.	n.a.	88.0	(3)	0.0	0.0
AHB	Australia	Honey	12 271	285 189	23 936	0.0	(3)	4.3	0.0	51.3	43.0	(3)	0.0	0.0
AHC	Australia	Apples	41 030	5 245 022	316 590	0.0	(3)	0.8	0.0	13.0	10.0	(3)	0.0	0.0
AHC	Australia	Avocado	178	254 829	17 376	0.0	(3)	0.1	0.0	1.0	-	(3)	0.0	0.0
AHC	Australia	Citrus, other	3 603	102 189	4 500	0.0	(3)	3.5	0.0	80.1	-	(3)	0.0	0.0
AHC	Australia	Pears	25 276	1 496 585	158 445	0.0	(3)	1.7	0.0	16.0	-	(3)	0.0	0.0
AMLC/MLA	Australia	Bovine meat	1 060 942	7 239 563	1 787 985	0.0	(3)	14.7	0.0	59.3	44.0	(3)	0.0	0.0
AMLC/MLA	Australia	Sheepmeat and goat												
AMLC/MLA	Australia	Lamb	232 825	863 842	598 861	0.0	(3)	27.0	0.0	38.9	45.0	(3)	0.0	0.0
QSC	Australia	Sugar (raw equivalent)	4 121 478	38 062 677	5 277 333	100.0	(1)	10.8	10.8	78.1	20.0	(2)	78.1	80.0
AWB	Australia	Wheat	14 150 262	123 204 300	19 571 500	100.0	(1)	11.5	11.5	72.3	-	(2)	72.3	86.0

Table II.18. Exporting STE: Average 1995-97 (cont.)

STE	Country	Product	National exports (MT)	World exports (MT)	Domestic production	Share of STE in national exports (%)	CEe case	Share of national exports in world exports (%)	Share of STE in world exports (%)	Share of national exports in domestic production (%)		MSp case	Share of STE in domestic procurement (%)	
			Ce	We	Pd	CEe =100 =0 0<Cee<100		Ce/We	CEe* (Ce/We)	Ce/Pd	Notification		MSp =100 =Cee*(Ce/Pd) +Sdm	Notification
GPWA	Australia	Barley	3 572 653	27 058 903	6 333 597	24.0	(1)	13.2	3.2	56.4	-	(2)	13.5	24.0
GPWA	Australia	Oilseeds (canola)	n.a.	n.a.	n.a.	17.0	(1)	n.a.	n.a.	n.a.	-	(2)	n.a.	17.0
NSWGB	Australia	Barley	3 572 653	27 058 903	6 333 597	17.0	(1)	13.2	2.2	56.4	-	(2)	9.6	17.0
NSWGB	Australia	Oats	200 817	2 810 735	1 703 667	34.0	(1)	7.1	2.4	11.8	-	(2)	4.0	17.0
NSWGB	Australia	Oilseeds (canola)	n.a.	n.a.	n.a.	46.0	(1)	n.a.	n.a.	n.a.	-	(2)	n.a.	17.0
NSWGB	Australia	Sorghum	295 469	6 519 208	1 430 087	29.0	(1)	4.5	1.3	20.7	-	(2)	6.0	17.0
RMB	Australia	Rice (milled)	624 930	20 969 237	719 486	100.0	(1)	3.0	3.0	86.9	-	(1)	100.0	100.0
WJ/WSAL	Australia	Wool (clean equivalent)	617 660	1 249 111	1 186 667	4.0	(2)	49.4	2.0	52.1	-	(3)	0.0	0.0
NZDB	New Zealand	Butter, Ghee	262 472	1 328 538	312 905	100.0	(1)	19.8	19.8	83.9	-	(2)	83.9	-
NZDB	New Zealand	Casein	n.a.	n.a.	n.a.	100.0	(1)	n.a.	n.a.	n.a.	-	(2)	n.a.	-
NZDB	New Zealand	Cheese	192 671	2 752 910	234 485	100.0	(1)	7.0	7.0	82.2	-	(2)	82.2	-
NZDB	New Zealand	Anhydrous milkfat/ghee	n.a.	n.a.	n.a.	100.0	(1)	n.a.	n.a.	n.a.	-	(2)	n.a.	-
NZDB	New Zealand	Milk, skimmed	2 936 010	22 119 330	4 620 100	100.0	(1)	13.3	13.3	63.5	-	(2)	63.5	-
NZDB	New Zealand	Milk, whole	2 249 772	20 420 643	10 115 667	100.0	(1)	11.0	11.0	22.2	-	(2)	22.2	-
HMB	New Zealand	Hops	668	45 303	789	100.0	(1)	1.5	1.5	84.7	-	(1)	100.0	100.0
KMB	New Zealand	Kiwi fruit	202 235	729 406	232 000	100.0	(1)	27.7	27.7	87.2	82.0	(2)	87.2	82.0

Table II.18. Exporting STE: Average 1995-97 (cont.)

STE	Country	Product	National exports (MT) Ce	World exports (MT) We	Domestic production Pd	Share of STE in national exports (%) CEe =100 =0 0<Cee<100	CEe case	Share of national exports in world exports (%) Ce/We	Share of STE in world exports (%) CEe* (Ce/We)	Share of national exports in domestic production (%) Ce/Pd	Notification	MSp case	Share of STE in domestic procurement (%) MSp =100 =Cee*(Ce/Pd)+Sdm	Notification
SFMR	Czech Rep	Wheat	524 077	123 204 300	3 730 080	0.0	(3)	0.4	0.0	14.1	-	(3)	0.0	-
SFMR	Czech Rep	Butter, Ghee	25 135	1 328 538	67 674	97.0	(2)	1.9	1.8	37.1	-	(3)	0.0	-
SFMR	Czech Rep	Cheese	14 368	2 752 910	113 490	52.0	(2)	0.5	0.3	12.7	-	(3)	0.0	-
SFMR	Czech Rep	Milk, skimmed	212 509	22 119 330	1 424 433	29.0	(2)	1.0	0.3	14.9	-	(3)	0.0	-
AMA	Poland	Wheat	163 548	123 204 300	8 478 890	20.0	(2)	0.1	0.0	1.9	-	(3)	0.0	13.0
AMA	Poland	Rye	11 236	2 509 706	5 746 545	20.0	(2)	0.4	0.1	0.2	-	(3)	0.0	13.0
AMA	Poland	Butter, Ghee	8 870	1 328 538	162 333	20.0	(2)	0.7	0.1	5.5	-	(3)	0.0	7.0-15.0
AMA	Poland	Milk, skimmed	1 323 269	22 119 330	3 635 000	20.0	(2)	6.0	1.2	36.4	-	(3)	0.0	18.0
CCC	United States	Coarse grains	53 650 225	67 292 677	229 152 667	0.1	(2)	79.7	0.1	23.4	-	(3)	0.0	-
CCC	United States	Butter, Ghee	25 093	1 328 538	547 482	77.0	(2)	1.9	1.5	4.6	-	(3)	0.0	-
CCC	United States	Milk, skimmed	697 161	22 119 330	8 895 493	98.0	(2)	3.2	3.1	7.8	-	(3)	0.0	-
CCC	United States	Cheese	35 997	2 752 910	3 588 090	15.0	(2)	1.3	0.2	1.0	-	(3)	0.0	-

NOTES

1.   These reports will be referred to as "previous studies."

2.   Part I discusses the need to consider the nature of the trading environment in which an STE operates in order to evaluate the potential for trade distortion. It also notes that it may be possible that private traders, in some instances, distort trade in similar ways to an STE. Indeed, some of the classification criteria used in this paper might be modified to apply to private traders as well. That private traders are not included reflects the modest goal of this paper, which is to gather and display in an organised way the information available on the different types of STEs in existence. It does not aim at providing an analysis of their trade distortionary potential, nor at comparing them with other trading entities.

3.   National agencies within the EU that purchase agricultural commodities when prices fall below a certain level, set by the Council of Ministers each year. The commodity stocks held by the intervention agencies may be sold on the EU market if prices rise above intervention levels, or exported using export restitutions (variable export subsidies to traders to cover the difference between the internal EU price and the world price). Intervention purchases are used primarily for the markets in cereals, butter and skimmed milk powder, and beef.

4.   Measures intended to stabilise markets, standardise quality and packaging, regulate flows to the market and authorise research and development for certain farm commodities; used in particular for fruits, vegetables and nuts. There is no direct control of pricing or production, however, specific forms of volume management such as producer allotments, market allocation and reserve pools, as well as market flow regulations such as handler prorates and shipping holidays can be viewed as conferring market power affecting competitive conditions. Orders are binding on the entire industry in the area regulated. The marketing order is requested by a group of producers and must be approved by the Secretary of Agriculture and a required number of the commodity's producers (usually two-thirds) in the area regulated. Orders are financed by production levies.

5.   B. Paddock (1998) p. 9 and M. Veeman *et al.* (1998), pp.10-17.

6.   For details, see WTO (1996) and (1998).

7.   M. Ingco and F. Ng (1998).

8.   WTO (1995).

9.   P. Dixit and T. Josling (1997)

10.   In this and the following paragraphs, the classifications developed by the authors of the different studies are reported without comment and it should not be interpreted as implying agreement or otherwise on the part of the authors of the present report.

11.   See K. Ackerman, P. Dixit and M. Simone (1997) for the exporting STE case and K. Ackerman (1997) for the importing STE case, respectively.

12.   M. Veeman, M. Fulton and B. Larue (1998).

13.   This study refers to OECD research (1996*a, b*) on contestability indicators.

14.   This study admits that the specification of market shares of 33% and 50% is judgmental and based on the industrial organisation specification of a dominant firm as one that controls 50% to 90% of market share (Shepherd, 1979).

15.   State Trading Enterprises can be classified in various ways. As the IPC (1999) pointed out, an STE may be involved in one or more of the following operations: importing, exporting, marketing products domestically, or a combination of two or more of these activities. From the IPC's point of view, the approach to confine the study only to importing STEs and exporting STEs may be criticised as it is based on too narrow a viewpoint. As reiterated above, however, this paper is intended to provide general information on the basis of simple, standardised criteria for comparison across STEs in various countries. As a consequence, focus was placed on the aspects of export and import. It cannot be denied, however, that there is difficulty in classifying some STEs as either exporting or importing cases because exclusive rights have been given for domestic market intervention purpose.

16.   Veeman *et al.*, Part III.2, p. 88.

17.   It should be noted that officially supported export credits may or may not be trade distorting, depending on the conditions under which they are granted. Officially supported export credits may be trade distorting is if they provide importers with financing more favourable than is offered by the private market and do not charge offsetting fees.

18.   A trade restriction involving a lower (in-quota) tariff rate for a specified volume of imports and a higher (over-quota) tariff rate for imports above the concessionary access level. Under the UR Agreement on Agriculture, most countries have agreed to progressive reductions in the over-quota tariff rates. Some countries have also agreed to lower the in-quota tariff rates and/or raise the concessionary access level.

19.   According to the UR Agreement on Agriculture, this means AMS calculated on a product-specific basis for each basic agricultural product receiving market price support, non-exempt direct payments, or any other subsidy not exempted from the reduction commitment. AMS differs from the Producer Support Estimate in many respects, the most important of which is that price gaps in the AMS calculation are estimated by reference to domestic administered prices and not actual producer prices, and that external reference prices are fixed at the average levels of the 1986-88 base period. In addition, many budgetary transfers which are included in PSEs are excluded from the AMS. From this difference, the PSE could be an alternative estimate of the domestic support level for specific commodities in the OECD countries. Currently, the PSE is limited to 13 basic commodities: wheat, maize, other grains, rice, oilseeds, sugar, milk, beef, pigmeat, poultry, sheepmeat, wool and eggs. This is the reason that preference is given to the product-specific AMS instead of the PSE.

20.   As explained, the WTO members have been requested to supply new and full notifications in 1995 and 1998. In particular, the WTO suggested in 1998 proposed a revised questionnaire that contains concrete and tangible information on state trading. However, as of November 1999 only the European Union, Iceland, Japan, Korea, New Zealand, Norway and Turkey of the OECD Member countries have notified in accordance with 1998 questionnaire. Thus, while priority is given to 1998 notifications, the notifications of 1995 and other years will be used as complements or substitutes in the absence of 1998 notifications.

21.   WTO (1998) does not deistiguish between these types.

BIBLIOGRAPHY

Australian Bureau Of Statistical (1999), "Australia Now — A Statistical Profile", http://www.abs.gov.au/websitedbs.

Australian Wheat Board (1999), "AWB Annual Report 1997-98", http://www.awb.com.au/corporate/e5501.htm.

Canadian Dairy Commission (1999a), "Canadian Dairy Commission: Overview", http://www.cdc.ca/glance.html.

Canadian Dairy Commission (1999b), "All about Canada's Dairy Industry", http://www.cdc.ca/general.html

Canadian Wheat Board (1999a), "About the Canadian Wheat Board", http://www.cwb.ca/publicat/about/about.htm

Canadian Wheat Board (1999b), "The Canadian Wheat Board 1997-1998 Annual Report", http://www.cwb.ca/publicat/annual/html98/start%20index.htm

Dixit, P. and T. Josling (1997), "State Trading in Agriculture: An Analytical Framework", *International Agricultural Trade Research Consortium Working Paper*, No. 97-4, July.

European Commission (EU 1998a), "Agricultural Situation and Prospects in the Central and Eastern European Countries: Czech Republic", *European Commission Directorate General for Agriculture (DG VI) Working Document*, May.

European Commission (EU 1998b), "Agricultural Situation and Prospects in the Central and Eastern European Countries: Poland", *European Commission Directorate General for Agriculture (DG VI) Working Document*, June.

Ingco, M. and F. Ng (1998), *Distortionary Effects of State Trading in Agriculture: Issues for the Next Round of Multilateral Trade Negotiations*, World Bank, February.

International Policy Council On Agriculture, Food And Trade (IPC 1999), "State Trading and the WTO: Reforming the Rules for Agriculture", *IPC Position Paper*, No.9.

Karen, A., P. Dixit and M. Simone (1997), "State Trading Enterprises: Their Role in World Markets", *Agricultural Outlook,* ERS, USDA,. June, pp. 11-16.

Karen, A. (1997), "State Trading Enterprises: Their Role As Importers", *Agricultural Outlook,* ERS, USDA., November, pp. 31-37.

Matsushita, M. (1998), "State Trading in Japan", *State Trading in the Twenty-First Century,* The University of Michigan Press, World Trade Forum, Vol. 1, ch.12.

New Southwales Grains Board (1999), http://www.nswgb.com.au.

New Zealand Apple And Pear Marketing Board (1999), *About ENZA,* http://www.enza.co.nz/2_about_enza.

New Zealand Dairy Board (1999*a*), "New Zealand Dairy Board-Facts-Company", http://www.nzmilk.co.nz/facts/company.html.

New Zealand Dairy Board (1999*b*), "New Zealand Dairy Board-Facts-International Dairy Market", http://www.nzmilk.co.nz/facts/figures-market.html.

New Zealand Meat Board. *et al.,* (1998), "New Zealand Red Meat Industry Strategic Direction: Towards 2006", paper prepared by New Zealand Red Meat Industry, February, http://www.nzmeat.co.nz/FILES/strategic%20direction.html..

OECD (1999), *National Policies and Agricultural Trade: Review of Agricultural Policies in Korea,* Paris.

OECD (1995*a*), *Review of Agricultural Policies: Czech Republic,* Paris.

OECD (1995*b*), *Review of Agricultural Policies: Poland,* Paris.

OECD, *Agricultural Policies in OECD Countries: Monitoring and Evaluation,* various years, Paris.

Paddock, B. (1998), "State Trading and International Trade Negotiations", Economic and Policy Analysis Directorate/Policy Branch, Agriculture and Agri-Food Canada (AAFC), December.

Shepherd, W. (1979), *The Economics of Industrial Organisation* (2nd ed.) Englewood Cliffs: Prentice-Hall Inc.

Sinclair, G. (1998), "Costs and Benefits of Producer Board Deregulation", *New Zealand Treasury Working Paper,* No.99-4, November.

United States Department Of Agriculture /Foreign Agricultural Service (USDA/FAS) (1998), The Competition in 1997: U.S. and Competitor Expenditures on Export Promotion and Export Subsidies for Agricultural,

Forestry and Fishery Products, *FAS' Perspective on World Export Policy Expenditures*, June.

Veeman, M., M. Fulton and B. Larue (1998), International Trade in Agricultural and Food Products: The Role of State Trading Enterprises, Agriculture and Agri-Food Canada (AAFC), *Trade Research Series*, November.

Woolstock Australia Limited (WSAL 1999), http://www.woolstock.aust.com.

Wood, D. (1998), "State Trading in the United States" in *State Trading in the Twenty-First Century*, The University of Michigan Press, World Trade Forum Vol. 1, ch.10.

WTO (1994), *The Results of the Uruguay Round of Multilateral Trade Negotiations: The Legal Texts.*

WTO (1995), *Operations of State Trading Enterprises as they Relate to International Trade*, background paper by the Secretariat, G/STR/2, 26 October, mimeo.

WTO (1996), *Draft Illustrative List: The Relationships between Governments and State Trading Enterprises and State Trading Activities*, paper by the USA, G/STR/W/32, 1 October, mimeo.

WTO (1998), "Draft Illustrative List of Relationships between Governments and State Trading Enterprises and the Kinds of Activities Engaged in by these Enterprises", paper by the Secretariat, G/STR/W/35, 27 July, mimeo.

WTO (1998), *Questionnaire on State Trading*, from the Working Party on State Trading Enterprises G/STR/3.

WTO (1999), *Illustrative List of Relationships Between Governments and State Trading Enterprises*, from the Working Party on State Trading Enterprises G/STR/4.

WTO, *Trade Policy Reviews*, various issues.

WTO, *Notifications on State Trading Enterprises by Member Countries,* various years.

WTO, *Notifications on Domestic Support by Member Countries,* various years.

WTO, *Notifications on Export Subsidy by Member Countries,* various years.